INFAMIES O[illegible]OUL
AND THEIR TR[illegible]ATMENTS

INFAMIES OF THE SOUL & THEIR TREATMENTS

'Uyūb al-nafs wa adwiyatuhā

Abū 'Abd al-Raḥmān
al-Sulamī

Translation & notes by
MUSA FURBER

ISBN 978-1-944904-10-4 (paper)
978-1-944904-11-1 (EPUB)

Published by:
Islamosaic
islamosaic.com

Cover image based on artwork © rogistok. I picked his image because, left untreated, the *nafs* is horrifying and toxic.

بسم الله الرحمن الرحيم

All praise is to Allah alone, the Lord of the Worlds
And may He send His benedictions upon
our master Muhammad, his Kin
and his Companions
and grant them
peace

TRANSLITERATION KEY

ء	ʾ (A distinctive glottal stop made at the bottom of the throat.)
ا	ā, a
ب	b
ت	t
ث	th (Pronounced like the *th* in *think*.)
ج	j
ح	ḥ (Hard *h* sound made at the Adam's apple in the middle of the throat.)
خ	kh (Pronounced like *ch* in Scottish *loch*.)
د	d
ذ	dh (Pronounced like *th* in *this*.)
ر	r (A slightly trilled *r* made behind the upper front teeth.)
ز	z
س	s
ش	sh
ص	ṣ (An emphatic *s* pronounced behind the upper front teeth.)
ض	ḍ (An emphatic *d*-like sound made by pressing the entire tongue against the upper palate.)
ط	ṭ (An emphatic *t* sound produced behind the front teeth.)
ظ	ẓ (An emphatic *th* sound, like the *th* in *this*, made behind the front teeth.)
ع	ʿ (A distinctive Semitic sound made in the middle of the throat and sounding to a Western ear more like a vowel than a consonant.)
غ	gh (A guttural sound made at the top of the throat resembling the untrilled German and French *r*.)
ف	f
ق	q (A hard *k* sound produced at the back of the palate.)
ك	k
ل	l
م	m
ن	n
ه	h (This sound is like the English *h* but has more body. It is made at the very bottom of the throat and pronounced at the beginning, middle, and ends of words.)
و	ū, u
ي	ī, i, y
ﷺ	A supplication made after mention of the Prophet Muḥammad, translated as "May Allah bless him and give him peace."

CONTENTS

PREFACE IX
AUTHOR'S INTRODUCTION 1
1. Expecting salvation despite violations 5
2. Comfort by the form of repentance 7
3. Fearing harm where none lies 9
4. Unconsciously slacking off in duties 10
5. Not feeling delight in ones duties 12
6. Expecting good while irritating others 13
7. Expecting success without any work 15
8. Truth and worship are contrary to its nature 17
9. Preferring vile notions 19
10. Preoccupation with the infamies of others 21
11. Heedlessness and negligence 23
12. Self-pity 25
13. Preoccupation with adorning the outward 26
14. Seeking compensation for its actions 27

15. Lacking delight in obedience 28
16. Laziness 29
17. Seeking leadership 30
18. Speaking often 32
19. Extravagant praise and censure 34
20. Discontentment with Allah's guidance 35
21. Wishing for the impossible 37
22. Being absorbed with worldly affairs 39
23. Showing off obedience 40
24. Avarice 41
25. Greed for the world 43
26. Approving only its own work 44
27. Pity towards the soul 45
28. Seeking revenge 46
29. Concern that one is honored 47
30. Concern for sustenance 48
31. Oft sinning 49
32. Grabbing attention while neglecting the self 51
33. Joy, happiness, and demanding comfort 53
34. Following caprice 54
35. Inclining towards fellowship 55
36. Vigor in obeying and approving of it 56

37. Following lusts 57
38. Feeling secure from Satan 58
39. Righteousness without sincerity 59
40. Blindness of Allah's respite 60
41. Spreading infamies of others 61
42. Lack of vigilance 62
43. Denigration and arrogance 63
44. Laziness and disregard for the law 65
45. Donning the garb of the righteous 66
46. Squandering time 67
47. Anger 68
48. Lying 69
49. Stinginess and miserliness 70
50. Its disposition for fancies 71
51. Being deluded by false praise 73
52. Avarice 73
53. Envy 74
54. Persisting in a sin while fancying mercy 75
55. Unwillingly performing acts of obedience 76
56. Avarice and being tightfisted 78
57. Accompanying the rebellious 79
58. Heedlessness 80

59. Idleness by feigning reliance on Allah 81
60. Departing knowledge for feigned achievements 82
61. Pride in what it gives 83
62. Showing need while having enough 84
63. Deeming itself superior 85
64. Toiling for its happiness 86
65. Ignorance of its creator's blessing 87
66. Grasping at dispensations 88
67. Disregarding lapses 89
68. Being deceived by miracles 90
69. Sitting with the rich 91
CONCLUSION 93
REFERENCES 94

PREFACE

INFAMIES OF THE SOUL AND THEIR TREATMENTS (*ʿUyūb al-nafs wa adwiyatuhā*) is one of the earliest manuals on the purification of the soul. It remains widely read within the Muslim world until today. Its author is Imām Abū ʿAbd al-Raḥmān Muḥammad ibn al-Ḥusayn ibn Muḥammad al-Sulamī (325–412 AH/937–1021 CE). Imām Abū ʿAbd al-Raḥmān al-Sulamī has authored over one hundred works. He is most famous for his works related to spiritual development and its masters, though he was also an accomplished scholar of the Shāfiʿī school of law, a hadith narrator, and a historian.

This book, *Infamies of the Soul,* contains sixty-nine infamies (wicked traits or actions) along with their treatments. The text includes many reports attributed to the Prophet ﷺ, his Companions (may Allah be pleased with them), the Successors, and others from the Pious Forbears (may Allah grant them all His mercy). Many of these reports are mentioned along with their chain of transmission. The chains and attributions are not always authentic, though the contents of the report tend to be accepted.

There are numerous editions of the book published in Arabic. I first learned about the book when

I received a copy from Sheikh Amīn al-Farūqī (may Allah protect him) who had prepared and annotated an edition that was published in Damascus by Dār Maktabat al-Beirūtī repeatedly in the mid-1990s. It was also published in Cairo in 1401/1981 by Dār al-Shurūq. It was published along with Aḥmad al-Zarrūq's versification in Beirut in 2010 by Dār al-Kutub al-ʿIlmiyyah. Etan Kohlberg published a critical edition in Jerusalem in 1976. Unfortunately, there is a great deal of variation between the editions which can confuse, distort, and change the meaning of the text.

I relied on Sheikh Amīn's edition for my first draft translation, which I then corrected against Kohlberg's and other editions. Aside from striving for an accurate translation of the text, I have also tried to track down the earliest sources for every quotation in the book, and I advise readers to consult the notes when quoting the book.

Where I have succeeded, it is only through the grace of Allah; where I have faltered it is from my own shortcomings. May Allah forgive the author, everyone mentioned in the book, its owners, readers, listeners, and all Muslims – living and dead.

MUSA FURBER
KUALA LUMPUR
NOVEMBER 8, 2018

AUTHOR'S INTRODUCTION

All praise belongs to Allah, first and last. May the blessings of Allah – outwardly and inwardly – always be upon Muḥammad and his folk, and many salutations.

All praise belongs to Allah who taught His elect [devotees] the infamies [bad qualities or wicked deeds] of their souls. He honored them with becoming acquainted with the treacheries of the soul, and He bestowed upon them awareness and attentiveness of the states that pass over it. He granted them success in remedying the soul's infamies and concealed evils, using remedies hidden [to all] except the attentive, resulting from their knowledge of the soul's sicknesses and busying themselves with remedies. And by this He thus made what is difficult easy for them, by His grace and success.

To proceed:

Some of the scholars (may Allah honor them with [acts of] obedience to Him) asked me to gather details about the infamies of the soul that can then be used to infer what [lies] behind it. I answered their request and gathered these details for him (And I ask Allah Most High that He not deprive us of their blessings!) after beseeching Allah for guidance and success. He is my sufficiency and what a wonderful helper! May the peace of Allah be upon Muḥammad, his folk and companions, and [His] many blessings.

So I say:

Know that the soul is of three types: the one that incites evil [*ammārah*], the reproachful soul [*lawwāmah*], and the one that is serene [*muṭma'innah*].

The *serene* soul is certain that Allah is its Lord, has found serenity in what Allah has promised, deemed true what Allah Most High has said, and is patient with His command. It is the faithful soul that Allah Most High has made luminous, has put its book [of deeds] into its right hand, and has purified. It is the soul that is content with the decree of Allah and its destiny: good and evil, beneficial and harmful. It is the soul to which Allah Most High says, "Return to your Lord pleased..." – with Allah – "...and pleasing" (Q89:28) – to others due to its righteous deeds and attesting the promise of Allah Most High.

The second [type of soul] is the *reproachful* soul. It reproaches good and evil, and is impatient [whether] things are easy or difficult. It regrets what it has missed and reproaches for [missing] it, saying, "If only I had done such-and-such," or "If only I had not done such-and-such." It is the immoral and rejected soul. Whenever this soul is dutiful or immoral it reproaches: if it does a good deed it says, "Why didn't I do more?," and if it does an evil deed it says, "If only I had not done that!" It reproaches itself in the Afterlife for squandering this life. It is the soul by which Allah Most High swore when He said, "And I shall swear by the reproaching soul" (Q75:2).

[The third is] the soul that incites evil, the one concerning which Allah Most High – when conveying [the story of] Yusūf (peace be upon him) – said, "The soul does indeed incite to evil" (Q12:53), [and elsewhere] "and curbed their souls' passions" (Q79:40), "Do you see he who has taken his passion for his god?" (Q45:23), and other verses which indicate the evils of the soul and its little desire for good.

ʿAlī ibn ʿAmr informed us, saying: ʿAbd al-Jabbār ibn Sirīn informed us, saying: Aḥmad ibn Ḥasan ibn Abān informed us, saying: Abū ʿĀsim informed us, saying: Shuʿbah and Sufyān informed [us] from Salmah ibn Kuḥayl: from Abū Salamah from Abū Hurayra (may Allah be pleased with him): the Prophet ﷺ said: "Tribulation, caprice, and lust are kneaded in the clay [constitution] of the sons of Adam."[1]

1. Ibn ʿAdī al-Jurjānī, *Al-Kāmil fī duʿafāʾ al-rijāl*, 1:324–325 #40. Ibn al-Jawzī, *Al-ʿIlal al-mutanāhiyah*, 1293; al-Kanānī, *Tanzīh al-sharīʿah al-marfūʿah*, 2:393; al-Dhahabī, *Mīzān al-iʿtidāl*, 1:89–90; al-Daylamī,

Allah Most High says, "And strive for Allah with the striving due to Him" (Q22:78) – meaning striving against the soul and preventing it from following caprice.

Al-Firdaus bi-maʿthūr, 7018; and al-Suyūṭī, *Al-Durr al-manthūr,* 1:117. All include a similar report, but without Abī Salamah. Their chains include Aḥmad ibn al-Ḥasan ibn Abān al-Miṣrī, who is said to have created and narrated forgeries.

1

EXPECTING SALVATION DESPITE VIOLATIONS

Among the infamies of the soul is its imagining that it is standing at the door of salvation, knocking with various litanies and good deeds while the door is open yet it has shut the door of returning [to the truth] on itself through numerous violations.

Al-Ḥusayn ibn Yaḥyā informed me, saying: I heard Jaʿfar ibn Muḥammad say: I heard Masrūq say:

> Rābiʿa al-ʿAdawiya passed by the assembly of Ṣāliḥ al-Murrī while Ṣāliḥ was saying, "Whoever persists in knocking on the door is on the verge of the door opening for him." Rābiʿa said, "The door, O underminer, is open but you flee from it! How can you reach a goal when you mistook its path from the first step?"[2]

---

2. There is a shorter version that ends with Ṣāliḥ saying, "A sheikh who is ignorant and a woman who is knowledgeable." Al-Sulamī, *Ṭabaqāt al-ṣūfiyyah*, 389; and al-Qushayrī, *Al-Risālat al-Qushayriyyah*, 2:425.

So how can the slave escape the infamies of the soul when he is the one who pursues passions for it? Or how can one escape from chasing whims when he does not hold back from violations?

I heard Muḥammad ibn Aḥmad ibn Ḥamdān say: I heard Muḥammad ibn Isḥāq al-Thaqafī say: I heard Ibn Abī al-Dunyā say, "One of the sages said, 'Do not expect to sober up while you have an infamy. And do not expect salvation while you have a sin [against you].'"[3]

This condition is treated by what Sarī al-Saqṭī said: [by] traveling the path of guidance, wholesome nourishment, and complete protection [from Allah].[4]

---

3. I have not located a source for this statement.
4. Al-Bayhaqī narrated it with a chain: Abū ʿAbd al-Raḥmān al-Sulamī reported, he said: I heard Muḥammad bin ʿAbd Allāh bin Shādhān say: I heard Bakr al-Ḥarbī say: I heard al-Sarī say: "Success is through three [things]: wholesome nourishment, complete protection, and the path of guidance." Al-Bayhaqī, *Al-Zuhd al-kabīr*, 935.

2

COMFORT BY THE FORM OF REPENTANCE

Among the infamies of the soul is that it is relieved and comforted whenever it cries.

This condition is treated by making grief [*kamad*] accompany crying, so the soul does not apply itself to feeling comforted. This is achieved by the individual humbly crying at [the moment of] sorrow [*ḥuzn*] – not crying from feeling sorrow, since whoever cries because of feeling sorrow finds comfort, while crying at the [moment of] sorrow increases one's grief [*kamad*] and sorrow [*ḥuzn*].

3

FEARING HARM WHERE NONE LIES

Among the infamies of the soul is its attempts to detect danger from someone who does not possess it, expecting benefit from someone incapable of it, and worrying about his sustenance [*rizq*] while it has been guaranteed to him.

This condition is treated by returning to [having] sound faith in what Allah reports in His book: "If Allah afflicts you with a misfortune none can remove it but He, and if He desires any good for you none can keep back His favor" (Q10:107), and His saying, "There is nothing walking the earth but its sustenance depends on Allah" (Q11:6).

Al-Aḥnaf ibn Qays was asked: "What made you the leader of your people, seeing how you are not the eldest?" He replied, "I was never negligent with responsibilities. And I never went overboard in something of which I had been relieved." And due to Allah Most High saying: "so worship Him and put your trust in Him" (Q11:123)."

This condition is rectified when one looks to the weakness and inability of people. Then the individual will know that everyone who is not self-sufficient [and depends on others] is incapable of fulfilling another's needs, and whoever is incapable is not able to carry out the material means of others. He will then be delivered from this infamy and return to his Lord in full.

4

UNCONSCIOUSLY SLACKING OFF IN DUTIES

Among the infamies of the soul is its slacking off in [religious] duties it used to perform. A greater infamy is when the individual is not concerned with his shortcomings and slacking off. Greater yet is when one is not even aware of his shortcomings and slacking off. And an even greater infamy is when one presumes he is thriving in spite of his shortcomings and slacking off.

This occurs from having little thanks during the occasions when the individual was successful in maintaining those [religious] duties. When his thanks grew little, he was removed from the station of plenty to the station of deficiency – and his deficiency was veiled to him so he then deemed the soul's vileness to be perfection. Allah Most High says, "Is he, the evil of whose deeds is made fair-seeming to him so that he deems it good [equal to one who is guided?]" (Q35:8), "[Those whose efforts have been wasted in the life of the world] while they thought they were doing good" (Q18:104), "[But they split their affair between them into groups,] each party rejoicing in what it has" (Q23:53), and "Thus unto every nation have We made their conduct seem fair" (Q6:108).

This infamy is removed by continually seeking refuge in Allah; adhering to making remembrance of Allah; reading His book [the Quran] and seeking out its meanings; venerating the sanctity of Muslims; and asking the friends of Allah [*awliyā'*] to pray for him that he return to the first state – perhaps Allah Mighty and Sublime will bestow upon him a blessing by opening to him a path to serve and obey Him.

5

NOT FEELING DELIGHT IN ONES DUTIES

Among the infamies of the soul is that it carries out religious duties while not finding delight therein. This is due to one's obedience being tainted with showing off, his lack of sincerity during obedience, or omitting one of the sunnas.

This condition is treated by demanding that the soul be sincere, by adhering to the sunnas in [one's] actions, and rectifying the initial stages of affairs so that their endings will be sound for him.

6

EXPECTING GOOD WHILE IRRITATING OTHERS

Among the infamies of the soul is that the individual expects good for himself by attending places where good things happen even though, if he did attend it, those present would lose hope and [consider] his presence an evil omen. One of the Forebears [*salaf*] was asked: "What is your expectation for those who stood [on ʿArafāt]?" He replied, "I see people whom Allah would forgive if it were not for me being with them."[5] This is what the People of Awareness [*ahl al-yaqaẓa*] assume about themselves.

This condition is treated by the individual knowing that Allah – even if He had forgiven one all his sins – has seen him commit mistakes and violations. He thus shies away from assuming good about himself and [instead] assumes the worst concerning himself. It is as al-Fuḍayl ibn Iyāḍ said, "How

5. Abū Bakr al-Muzanī said this to his son while making Ḥajj. Al-Daynūrī, *Al-Mujālasah wa jawāhir al-ʿilm*, 2697; al-Bayhaqī, *Shuʿab al-īmān*, 7903; Abū Ḥātim al-Dārimī, *Rawḍat al-ʿuqalāʾ*, 60; Yaḥyā bin Maʿīn, *Tārīkh Ibn Maʿīn*, 4570; Ibn Rajab, *Laṭāʾif al-maʿārif*, 285.

shameful of you – even if you are pardoned!"[6] This was because he realized Allah's knowledge of and His looking to him.

---

6. Isḥāq bin Ibrāhīm al-Ṭabarī reported al-Fuḍayl said this at ʿArafāt while making Ḥajj. Al-Aṣbahānī, *Ḥilyat al-awliyā'*, 8:88; al-Bayhaqī, *Shuʿab al-īmān*, 3897; al-Ghazālī, *Iḥyā' ʿulūm al-dīn*, 4:184; Ibn al-Jawzī, *Al-Tabṣirah*, 2:142; Ibn Rajab, *Laṭā'if al-maʿārif*, 285; Ibn ʿAsākir, *Tārīkh Dimashq*, 48:421; al-Dhahabī, *Siyar aʿlām al-nubalā'*, 7:400, 8:432.

7

EXPECTING SUCCESS WITHOUT ANY WORK

Among the infamies of the soul is that you will not bring your soul to life until you bring about its death. That is: You will not bring it to live for the Afterlife until you cause its death from this world. And you will not bring it to life through Allah until it is dead from delusions.

Yayḥā ibn Muʿādh [al-Rāzī] said, "Whoever draws closer to Allah by annihilating his soul, Allah will protect him from his soul."[7] This is [achieved] by denying the soul its lusts and compelling it to do what it dislikes.

The Prophet ﷺ said, "Paradise is surrounded by [the pursuit of] dislikes; Hellfire is surrounded by temptations."[8]

This condition is treated by staying up late at night [in worship], in addition to hunger, thirst, do-

7. Al-Sulamī, *Ṭabaqāt al-ṣūfiyyah,* 79; al-Shaʿrānī, *Al-Ṭabaqāt al-kubrā,* 1:61.
8. Muslim, 2823; Al-Tirmidhī, 2559. The hadith indicates the nature of types of actions that enter one into Paradise or the Hellfire.

ing things contrary to the soul's nature, and denying it its lusts. I heard Muḥammad ibn Ibrāhīm ibn al-Faḍl say: I heard Muḥammad ibn al-Rūmī say: I heard Yayḥā ibn Muʿādh al-Rāzī say: "Hunger is food through which Allah strengthens the bodies of the trusting ones [*ṣiddīqīn*]."[9]

9. Attributed to ʿAbd Allāh al-Kharrāz, who passed away before 310AH: al-Khaṭīb al-Baghdādī, *Al-Zuhd wa al-raqā'iq,* 105; al-Qushayrī, *Al-Risālah al-Qushayriyyah,* 1:105; al-Sulamī, *Ṭabaqāt al-ṣūfiyyah,* 223; al-Shaʿrānī, *Al-Ṭabaqāt al-kubrā,* 1:84. A similar and longer statement is attributed to Yaḥyā bin Muʿādh: Al-Aṣbahānī, *Ḥilyat al-awliyā',* 10:67.

8

TRUTH AND WORSHIP ARE CONTRARY TO ITS NATURE

Among the infamies of the soul is that it never prefers the truth, and worship is contrary to its nature and disposition. Most of this is derived from pursuing caprice and chasing desires. Anything that has not been slaughtered with the knives of disciplining the soul [*mujāhadat*] will not be brought to life. Allah Most High said to one group from the Children of Israel, "*so turn in penitence to your Creator and slay yourselves*" (Q2:54).

This condition is treated by removing the soul [from this world and dedicating it] to its Lord. Because of this, al-Khalīl [Ibrāhīm] (peace be upon him) was ordered to sacrifice his son, and "Then, when they had both surrendered to Allah, and he had turned him down on his face" it was said to him, "You have fulfilled the vision," and "We ransomed him with a tremendous sacrifice" (Q37:103, 105, 107).

Junayd said, "Allah has made affection unlawful to those with attachment [to this world]."[10]

The goal of the treatment is to completely remove the soul [from these attachments and to dedicate it solely] to its Lord.

I heard Muḥammad ibn ʿAbd Allāh al-Rāzī say: I heard Abū al-Qasim al-Baṣrī in Baghdad say:

Ibn Yazdāniyār was asked about a servant: "When he departs for his Lord on what basis should he set out?" He replied, "On [the basis] that he not return to where he departed, and that he safeguard his soul from noticing what he has absolved himself from."

Then someone asked, "This is the ruling for one who departs from something that is present. But what about someone who departs from something that is absent?" He said, "The presence of sweetness in the future [through dedication to one's Lord] in exchange for the bitterness of the past [and one's dedication to fantasy and folly]."[11]

---

10. Al-Aṣbahānī, *Ḥilyat al-awliyāʾ*, 10:274; al-Ghazālī, *Iḥyāʾ ʿulūm al-dīn*, 4:360.
11. Al-Qushayrī, *Al-Risālah al-Qushayriyyah*, 1:213.

9

PREFERRING VILE NOTIONS

Among the infamies of the soul is that it prefers vile, evil notions that order it to perform violations. This is from one's lack of vigilance [*murāqabah*] and lack of consistency in their remembrance of Allah.[12]

This condition is treated by resisting evil notions from the start so that they do not become ingrained. This is [achieved] by continual remembrance [of Allah], adhering to fear [of Him], and by knowing that Allah is aware of what is in your heart – just as created beings know what you make public. Hence you become shy from mending for creatures the place they view while you have not rectified the place the Real [Allah] views. The Prophet ﷺ said: "Allah does not look to your forms nor to your actions; rather, He looks to your hearts."[13]

---

12. This last sentence is from Aḥmad al-Zarrūq, *Urjūzat ʿUyūb al-nafs,* 44.
13. The text has "...nor to your actions...." Al-Bayhaqī reported that some groups of people repeated this often, even though its transmission was not established and it disagrees with the "...or your wealth..." which was transmitted via authentic chains. Al-Bayhaqī, *Al-*

I heard Abū Bakr al-Rāzī say: I heard Abū al-Ḥasan al-ʿAlawī, the companion of Ibrāhīm al-Khawwāṣ, say: I heard Ibrāhīm al-Khawwāṣ (may Allah grant him His mercy) say:

> The beginning of sin is the evil notion. If its owner does not obviate it by disliking it, it will become resistance. If its owner does not obviate it by resisting it, it becomes whispering. If its owner does not correct it through discipline, from it will awaken lusts with [his] capriciousness, and it will obstruct one's mind, knowledge, and clear distinction.

This is how it was transmitted in [non-prophetic] traditions: That whims and lusts overwhelm knowledge, intellect, and clear distinction.[14]

Asmā' wa al-ṣifāt, 1003; Muslim, 2564; Ibn Mājah, 4143.

14. Attributed to al-Ḥārith al-Muḥāsibī in Al-Aṣbahānī, *Ḥilyat al-awliyā',* 10:88.

10

PREOCCUPATION WITH THE INFAMIES OF OTHERS

Among the infamies of the soul is its being preoccupied with the infamies of others while being blind to its [own] infamies. ‹This comes from its arrogance, conceit, and heedlessness towards punishable deeds. And Allah Most High has said, "Woe to every scorner and mocker," (Q104:1).[15]›

This condition is treated by the individual seeing the infamy of his soul, his own knowledge of his soul, and his awareness of its machinations. One treats it by journeying, dedicating oneself, and accompanying the righteous and following their commands. If one does not work at treating the infamies of his [own] soul, then at the very least he is to remain silent concerning the infamies of others, excuse them for their infamies, and cover them up – out of hope that through this, Allah will rectify his infamies. The Prophet ﷺ said, "Whoever conceals his brother's shame, Allah will conceal his shame."[16] And the Prophet ﷺ said, "Whoever

15. Aḥmad al-Zarrūq, *Urjūzat ʿUyūb al-nafs*, 46.
16. This particular wording: al-Dāraquṭnī, *Al-ʿIlal al-*

pursues his Muslim brother's shame, Allah seeks his shame and then compromises him – even if he were within the hollows of his house."[17]

I heard Muḥammad ibn ʿAbd Allāh ibn Shādhān say: I heard Yazdān al-Madāʾinī say, "I saw groups of people who possessed infamies, yet they remained silent concerning the infamies of others and so Allah veiled their infamies [from others] and removed their infamies. And I saw people that did not have infamies and then became occupied with the infamies of others, and so they came to have infamies ."[18]

---

wāridah fī al-aḥādīth al-nabawiyyah, 10:186–88. Very similar wording is found in Ibn Mājah, 2546.

17. Al-Tirmidhī, 2032.
18. Similar statements are attributed to others. It is attributed to Mālik bin Anas: ʿAbd Allāh al-Ḥamīdī, *Akhbār wa ashʿār,* 380–81; ʿAbd Allāh al-Ḥamīdī, *Al-Tadhkirah,* 380–81; Muḥammad Amīn bin Faḍl Allāh, *Khulāṣat al-athar fī aʿyān al-qarn al-ḥādī ʿashar,* 4:195.
    Attributed to Ibn ʿUmar: al-Daylamī, *Al-Firdaws bi maʿthūrat al-khiṭāb,* 4830.
    Attributed to Abū Ḥātim al-Rāzī: al-Jurjānī, *Tārīkh Jurjān,* 252.

11

HEEDLESSNESS AND NEGLIGENCE

The infamies of the soul include: heedlessness, negligence, persistence [in bad deeds], procrastination, expecting the impossible, and a false sense of immortality.

The treatment for these conditions is what I heard al-Ḥusayn ibn Yayḥā say: I heard Jaʿfar al-Khuldī say:

> Junayd was asked, "What is the path [one follows] to dedicating oneself to Allah?"
>
> He answered: "Through repentance that dissolves persistence [in a sin], fear that ends procrastination, hope that incites action, remembering Allah during all variety of times, and through enfeebling the soul by making [it see] death [as] near and false-hopes distant."
>
> He was asked, "What means does the slave use to reach that?"

He answered, "Through a lonely heart containing pure *tawḥīd* [sound belief in monotheism]."[19]

19. Al-Istānbūlī, *Rūḥ al-bayān,* 2:39, 9:457; Ibn ʿAjībah, *Al-Baḥr al-madīd,* 5:76.

12

SELF-PITY

Among the infamies of the soul is its worrying about and pitying itself.

This condition is treated by the individual seeing the grace of Allah Most High that is upon one at all times and circumstance, in order to remove him from pitying his soul. I heard Abū Bakr al-Rāzī say: I heard al-Wāsiṭī (may Allah grant him His mercy) say, "The thing closest to the disgust of Allah is having pity for [*ru'yah*] the soul and its actions."[20]

---

20. Abū Bakr al-Rāzī reported that Abū al-ʿAbbās bin ʿAṭā' was asked this. Al-Aṣbahānī, *Ḥilyat al-awliyā'*, 10:303; al-Sulamī, *Al-Futuwwah*, 18; Ibn al-Jawzī, *Ṣifat al-ṣafwah*, 1:533.

13

PREOCCUPATION WITH ADORNING THE OUTWARD

Among the infamies of the soul is being preoccupied with adorning outward things, feigning humility without being humble, and feigning servitude without presence [of heart].

This condition is treated by being occupied by protecting their heart so that the light of one's inward [reality] adorns his visible deeds, and thus be adorned without adornment, dignified without an entourage, and mighty without a tribe. Because of this, the Prophet ﷺ said, "Whoever mends his heart, Allah will mend his public [deeds]."[21]

---

21. This is reported as something that scholars would say or write to one another: Ibn Abī al-Dunyā, *Al-Ikhlāṣ wa al-niyyah,* 25; Ibn Taymiyyah, *Majmūʿ al-fatāwā,* 7:9–10; Ibn al-Mufliḥ, *Al-Ādāb al-sharʿiyyah,* 1:136.

14

SEEKING COMPENSATION FOR ITS ACTIONS

Among the infamies of the soul is seeking compensation for its actions.

This condition is treated by the individual seeing his shortcomings in his deeds and his lack of sincerity. Indeed, the person who is astute about his actions turns away from compensations out of etiquette and piety, and knowing that what is appointed for him will come to him in this world and the next, and that nothing but sincerity can remove him from whatever is against him.

15

LACKING DELIGHT IN OBEDIENCE

Among the infamies of the soul is not finding delight in acts of obedience; this is from the heart's sickness and the soul's deception.[22]

This condition is treated by eating the lawful, continuously making remembrance [of Allah], serving the righteous and keeping close to them. During all of this, one beseeches Allah to bless one's heart with rectification by removing the manifold darkness of sicknesses, thus finding delight in acts of obedience.

22. See also #5.

16

LAZINESS

Among the infamies of the soul is laziness. It is the offspring of eating one's fill. When the soul is satiated it becomes strengthened, and when it is strengthened it takes its share. And when it takes its share it overpowers the heart and delivers it to its pleasures.

This condition is treated by inducing hunger, since when the soul is hungry it lacks pleasure. And when it lacks its pleasure it becomes weak. When the soul becomes weak, the heart [*qalb*] overpowers it. And when the heart overpowers the soul, the heart propels it to obey and removes laziness from it. Because of this the Prophet ﷺ said, "The Children of Adam do not fill a a vessel worse than their stomachs. All a child of Adam needs is a few bites to keep his back straight. But if need be, [it should be] one third for food, one third for drink, and one third for him to breathe."[23]

23. Al-Tirmidhī, 2380 – well-rigorously authenticated; Ibn Mājah, 3349.

17

SEEKING LEADERSHIP

Among the infamies of the soul is seeking leadership through knowledge, taking pride in and boasting about knowledge, and competing in knowledge with others of his kind.

This condition is treated by the individual seeing Allah's grace upon him in making him a vessel for [knowledge of] His judgments, and seeing the deficiency of his thanks for the bounties of Allah Most High of knowledge and wisdom. [Part of its treatment is] adhering to modesty and broken-heartedness, having compassion toward people and sincerely advising them. It was narrated that the Prophet ﷺ said, "Whoever seeks knowledge so he can contest with fools, vie with the scholars, or attract attention toward himself, occupies his seat in the Fire."[24]

Because of this, one of the Successors said,

24. This report has multiple chains. The chain from Ḥudhayfa (may Allah be pleased with him): Ibn Mājah, 259. The chain from Kaʿb (may Allah be pleased with him): Al-Tirmidhī, 656. It is also included in al-Dārimī, 374. The hadith has supporting chains, see *Majmaʿ al-zawāʾid*, 1:183-84.

"Whoever increases in knowledge increases in fear,"[25] since Allah Most High said, "Only the learned among His servants fear Allah" (Q35:28).

A man called [out to] al-Shaʿbī, "O scholar!" He replied, "The scholar is the one who fears Allah ."[26]

---

25. Ibn Qayyim al-Jawziyyah, *Ṭarīqat al-hijratayn,* 283; Abū Saʿīd al-Khādimī, 1:279; Ibn Rajab, *Faḍl ʿIlm al-Salaf.*
26. Al-ʿIrāqī, et al, *Takhrīj aḥādīth Iḥyāʾ ʿulūm al-dīn,* 1:215; Ibn Taymiyyah, *Al-Ḥasanah wa al-sayyiʾah*, 63; Ibn Taymiyyah, *Jāmiʿ al-masāʾil*, 1:131; Ibn Taymiyyah, *Majmūʿ al-fatāwā,* 3:333, 7:539, 14:292, 16:179; Ibn al-Qayyim al-Jawziyyah, *Shifāʾ al-ʿalīl*, 172; Abū Saʿīd al-Khādimī, *Barīqah Muḥammadiyyah*, 2:210.
The statement was also attributed to others, including Sufyān al-Thawrī and al-Awzāʿī: al-Aṣbahānī, *Ḥilyat al-awliyāʾ*, 3:63; Ibn ʿAbd al-Barr, *Jāmiʿ bayān al-ʿilm wa faḍlihi*, 1:691, 1211; Yaḥyā bin Ḥussein al-Shajarī, *Tartīb al-amālī al-khumaysiyyah,* 308.

18

SPEAKING OFTEN

Among the infamies of the soul is talking too often. This is born from two things: seeking leadership and wanting people to see one's knowledge and eloquence, or not knowing what [punishable consequences] speaking brings him.

This condition is treated by the individual realizing that he is held accountable for what he says, that what he says is recorded against him and that he is held responsible for it. Allah Most High says, "Yet there are guardians watching over you, Noble recorders" (Q82:10-11), and He Most High said, "Each word he utters is noted by a vigilant guardian" (Q50:18).

The Prophet ﷺ said, "Whoever believes in Allah and the Afterlife [should either] say something good or remain silent."[27] And the Messenger of Allah ﷺ said, "Verily, utterances are the harbinger of catastrophe,"[28] and he ﷺ said, "And are people

27. Al-Bukhārī, 6018; Muslim, 47 #74.

28. It is attributed to the Prophet ﷺ in Abū Bakr al-Kalabādhī, *Baḥr al-fawā'id*, 119; Abū 'Abd Allāh al-Qaḍā'ī, *Musnad al-Shihāb*, 227, 228; al-Bayhaqī, *Shu'ab al-īmān,* 4597, 4598; Ibn Abī al-Dunyā, *Al-Ṣamt,* 286; Ibn Abī al-Dunyā, *Dhamm al-ghībah*, 150; Abū al-Shaykh al-Aṣbahānī, *Amthāl al-ḥadīth*, 50.

thrown down on their nostrils in the Hellfire except by what their tongues reap?!"[29] and he ﷺ said, "The speech of the Children of Adam is against him, not for him – unless it be commanding the good, forbidding evil, or remembrance of Allah."[30] This is taken from Allah Mighty and Majestic saying, "No good is there in much of their private conversation, except for those who enjoin charity or that which is right or conciliation between people" (Q4:114).

29. Ibn Jārūd al-Ṭayālisī, *Musnad Abī Dāwūd al-Ṭayālisī*, 561; Ibn Abī Shaybah, *Al-Muṣannaf*, 26498; Aḥmad bin Ḥanbal, *Al-Musnad*, 22063, 22068; al-Ḥārith al-Muḥasibī, *Ādāb al-nufūs*, 43.
30. ʿAbd al-Ḥamīd bin Ḥumayd, *Al-Muntakhab*, 1552; al-Tirmidhī, 2412 – *ḥasan gharīb*; Ibn Mājah, 3974.

19

EXTRAVAGANT PRAISE AND CENSURE

Among the infamies of the soul is that when it is pleased, it praises the one with whom it is pleased beyond the [proper] limits; and when it is angered it censures and exceeds the [proper] limits.

This condition is treated by disciplining the soul on candor and truthfulness until it does not transgress in praising whomever it is pleased with, and does not censure the one with whom it is angry. This is because most of this [excess] is from the lack of regard for orders and prohibitions. Allah Most High said, "Do not follow that of which you have no knowledge, for [man's] eyes, ears and heart, each of these shall be questioned about this" (Q17:36). The Prophet ﷺ said, "Toss dirt in the faces of those who praise excessively."[31]

---

31. Muslim, 3002 #68; al-Tirmidhī, 2393; Abū Dāwūd, 4804; al-ʿIrāqī, et al, *Takhrīj aḥādīth Iḥyāʾ ʿulūm al-dīn*, 2825.

20

DISCONTENTMENT WITH ALLAH'S GUIDANCE

Among the infamies of the soul is that it seeks guidance from Allah Most High for its actions, and then becomes angry with what He chooses.

This condition is treated by the individual knowing that he knows the outward appearance of things while Allah knows what lies within and their reality. [And by him knowing] that the excellence of what Allah chose for him is better than what he chooses for himself since no slave chooses a circumstance for himself save that it is enfolded with tribulation. Hence, the individual realizes that he is planned and not a planner, and that his discontent with the One who Decrees does not change the decree. So he adheres to the way of accepting the decree of Allah and becomes comforted.

The Prophet ﷺ said, "There is not a single person save that he has sustenance that will come to him. Whoever is satisfied with his sustenance is blessed in it and it suffices him. But whoever is not satisfied with it will not be blessed in it and it will not suffice him."[32]

32. I have not located a source for this statement.

Among the Prophets (Dāwūd or another [peace be upon them all]) said, "O my Lord. Who is the most evil of your slaves?" He, Majestic is His Majesty, replied, "Whoever is not satisfied with My judgment."[33]

33. Al-Diyār Bakrī, *Tārīkh al-khamīs fī aḥwāl anfus al-nafīs,* 1:18.

21

WISHING FOR THE IMPOSSIBLE

Among the infamies of the soul is often wishing for the impossible. Wishing for the impossible is resisting Allah Most High in His decree and [what He] destines.

The treatment for this condition is the individual knowing that he does not discern the consequence of his wishing: will it compel him toward good or evil, and towards what he agrees with or what angers him. When he ascertains the uncertain outcome of his wishing, it departs his soul and he returns to acceptance and surrender, and he finds comfort. Because of this, the Prophet ﷺ said, "If one of you makes a wish: he must examine what he wishes for, since you know not which of your wishes is written for you,"[34] and he ﷺ said, "Let not a single one of you wish for death from a harm

34. Aḥmad bin Ḥanbal, *Al-Musnad,* #8689; al-Bukhārī, *Al-Adab al-Mufrad,* 794; Ibn Abī al-Dunyā, *Al-Mutamannīn,* 151; Ibn ʿAdī al-Jurjānī, *Al-Kāmil fī ḍuʿafāʾ al-rijāl,* 6:77; al-Bayhaqī, *Shuʿab al-īmān,* 6889; Ibn Mufliḥ, *Al-Ādāb al-sharʿiyyah,* 2:96.

that befalls him. One is to say: ‘O Allah, grant me life as long as living is better for me, and grant me death if death is better for me.’”[35]

35. Al-Bukhārī, 5671; Muslim, 2680 #10.

22

BEING ABSORBED WITH WORLDLY AFFAIRS

Among the infamies of the soul is that it loves being absorbed in the ways of the world and whatever people speak about.

This condition is treated by the individual being occupied with maintaining remembrance [of Allah] at all times so that it busies one from remembering this world and its folk, and [from] being absorbed with their occupations. And [it is treated by] one knowing that these are among the things that do not concern him and thus leaves them, since the Prophet ﷺ said, "Among perfecting a person's Islam is leaving that which does not concern him."[36]

36. Ibn Mājah, 3976; al-Tirmidhī, 2317-18.

23

SHOWING OFF OBEDIENCE

Among the infamies of the soul is showing its obedience, its love that people know about or see him being obedient, and their having the opinion that he is adorned with obedience.

This condition is treated by the individual knowing that he does not possess any benefit or harm to [other] people, and that he struggle in demanding sincerity from his soul in performing its deeds in order to bring an end to this infamy. Allah Most High says, "And they have been ordered no more than this: To worship Allah sincerely, being True [in faith]" (Q98:5).

The Prophet ﷺ said, conveying from his Lord Mighty and Majestic, "Whoever performs any deed [wherein he] associates someone else with Me: I am free of it and it belongs to the one he associated with Me."[37]

37. Muslim, 2985 #46.

24

AVARICE

Among the infamies of the soul is avarice.

This condition is treated by the individual knowing that his avarice enters him into this world, makes him forget the sweetness of worship, and enslaves him to [those who are themselves] slaves after Allah made him free from their enslavement. The Prophet ﷺ sought protection and said, "I seek refuge in You from avarice that leads to [more] avarice, and from avarice for that which is not desirous"[38] – which is a [type of] avarice that Allah etched on the heart which urges one to be desirous of this world and to do little for the Afterlife.

It was related from one of the Forebears (may Allah be merciful with them) that he said, "Coveting is poverty that is present."[39] An affluent person who covets is poor; and the poor, modest person

38. Al-Ṭabarānī, *Al-Duʿā'*, 1387; al-Ṭabarānī, *Musnad al-shāmiyyīn,* 1872; Ibn Abī al-Dunyā, *Al-Qināʿah wa al-taʿffuf,* 190; al-Haythamī, *Ghāyat al-maqṣad*, 4744; al-Ḥaythamī, *Majmaʿ al-zawā'id,* 17181–82.

39. Al-Rūyānī, *Al-Musnad,* 1538; al-Ṭabarānī, *Al-Muʿjam al-awsaṭ,* 7753; Abū al-Shaykh al-Aṣbahānī, *Amthāl al-ḥadīth*, 226; al-Ḥākim, *Al-Mustadrak,* 4:362, §7928; al-ʿIrāqī, *Al-Mugnī ʿan ḥaml al-asfār,* 1392.

is rich. Coveting is what breaks necks, humiliates (lit. "blackens faces"), and kills hearts.

[It is reported that] Allah Most High says, "I did not make one being subservient to another, except in making one subservient to his wishes. Had no one hoped for someone other than Me, I wouldn't have given one being authority over another."[40]

A poet said:

> (How) do you covet Layla yet you know that
>
> (it is) the coveted things that break men's necks?![41]

As well as:

> I obeyed the things I coveted and they enslaved me
>
> If only I had been satisfied, I would have been free.[42]

---

40. I have not located a source for this statement.

41. Al-Sulamī, *Ṭabaqāt al-ṣūfiyyah*, 231; Ibn Mulaqqin, *Ṭabaqāt al-awliyā'*, 385. A more-frequently mentioned version of the line is:

    I coveted Layla that she return

    Only coveted things break men's necks!

    cf Ibn al-Fāris, *Maqāyīs al-lughghah*, 2:468.

42. Al-Ḥallāj is reported to have sung this when being killed. Ibn Taymiyyah, *Al-ʿUbūdiyyah*, 81; Ibn Taymiyyah, *Al-Fatāwā al-kubrā*, 5:179; Ibn Taymiyyah, *Majmūʿ al-fatāwā*, 10:181, 18:329; Ibn al-Mufliḥ, *Al-*

25

GREED FOR THE WORLD

Among the infamies of the soul is greed for prolonging its stay in this world and increasing [his share of] it.

This condition is treated by the individual knowing that this world is not a permanent abode for him and knowing that the abode of the next life is permanent. Someone who is rational works for his permanent abode, not for the stages of his journey. Indeed, the stages [of travel] come to an end while residency in [one's] destination endures, and so one works for where his destination lies. Allah Most High says, "Know that the life of this world is only play, and diversion, and adornment, and boasting among you, and rivalry in respect of wealth and children" (Q57:20). And [one works for the permanent abode] because Allah Most High says, "While the Hereafter is better and longer lasting" (Q87:17), and He Most High said, "The Hereafter is better for those who fear [Allah]" (Q6:35).

Ādāb al-sharʿiyyah, 3:309; Ibn Kathīr, *Al-Bidāyah wa al-nihāyah,* 11:142; Ibn Khalikān, *Wafāyāt al-aʿyān,* 2:144; al-Dhahabī, *Siyar aʿlām al-nubalāʾ,* 14:346.

26

APPROVING ONLY ITS OWN WORK

Among the infamies of the soul is that it considers its own bad deeds to be beautiful, and deems the actions of whoever disagrees with him to be ugly.

This condition is treated by impeaching the soul since the soul is the [thing which is] predisposed to evil, and [by] assuming the best concerning people because [final] outcomes are unknown.

27

PITY TOWARDS THE SOUL

Among the infamies of the soul is taking pity on the soul and supporting whatever it advocates.[43]

This condition is treated by the individual turning away from the soul, and paying little attention to it. I heard my grandfather [Abū ʿAmr Ismāʿīl bin Nujayd] (may Allah grant him His mercy) say, "An individual who holds himself in high esteem places little importance in his religion [*dīn*]."[44]

43. See #12.
44. Al-Bayhaqī, *Al-Zuhd al-kabīr,* 331, 733; al-Qushayrī, *Al-Risālah al-Qushayriyyah,* 1:217; al-Sulamī, *Ṭabaqāt al-ṣūfiyyah,* 340; al-Shaʿrānī, *Al-Ṭabaqāt al-kubrā,* 1:102–3.

28

SEEKING REVENGE

Among the infamies of the soul is that one seeks revenge, argues, and gets angry for its sake.

This condition is treated by the individual feeling enmity towards the soul and despising it, loving revenge for the sake of the religion, and having anger for perpetrating prohibitions. It was related that the Prophet ﷺ never retaliated for his sake, but if the sanctity of Allah was violated he would retaliate for Allah – then he would retaliate for the sake of Allah.[45]

---

45. Al-Bukhārī, 3560; Muslim, 2327 #77.

29

CONCERN THAT ONE IS HONORED

Among the infamies of the soul is being occupied with rectifying the outward for [the sake of] onlookers, and its heedlessness of mending the inward, which is what Allah Mighty and Majestic watches [and is more deserving of rectification].

This condition is treated by the individual ascertaining that people honor him only to the extent that Allah has put in their hearts, and his knowing that the inward is where Allah watches – hence mending the inner is more proper than mending the outward which is where people look. Allah Most High says, "Allah is Watching over you" (Q4:1).

The Prophet ﷺ said, "Allah does not look to your forms nor to your deeds. Rather, He looks to your hearts and your intentions."[46]

---

46. See also #9.

30

CONCERN FOR SUSTENANCE

Among the infamies of the soul is its concern for sustenance even though Allah has guaranteed it for the individual, and its lack of concern for the work that Allah has made obligatory for him that no one else can do for him.

This condition is treated by the individual knowing that Allah, the One who created him, has guaranteed for him sufficient sustenance, and said, "Allah is He Who created [you], then provided for you" (Q30:40). Just as one does not doubt His creation, one does not doubt His provision.

I heard Muḥammad ibn ʿAbd Allāh say: it is conveyed from Ḥātim al-Aṣamm that he said: "There is no morning except Satan says [to me]: 'Today, what will you eat? What will you wear? Where will you sleep?' I reply to him: 'I will eat death, I will wear my burial shroud, I will sleep in the grave.'"[47]

---

47. Al-Istānbūlī, *Rūḥ al-bayān,* 7:154; Al-Aṣbahānī, *Ḥilyat al-awliyā',* 10:49; Ibn al-Jawzī, *Ṣifat al-ṣafwah,* 2:340.

31

OFT SINNING

Among the infamies of the soul is its sins and violations being so numerous that the heart becomes hard.

This condition is treated by seeking much forgiveness and repenting with every breath; perpetually fasting and praying at night; serving good people; sitting with the righteous; and attending assemblies of remembrance. A man complained to the Prophet ﷺ about the hardness of his heart, and he ﷺ replied, "Bring him near the assemblies of remembrance."[48]

[In addition,] the Prophet ﷺ said, "Indeed, I seek forgiveness from Allah seventy times during the day."[49]

He ﷺ said: "When the servant sins, a black speck spots his heart. If he repents and seeks forgiveness from Allah, the speck departs. If he sins a second time, another speck spots his heart. [This happens]

---

48. This is attributed to al-Ḥasan al-Baṣrī. Al-Kharā'iṭī, *I'tilāl al-qulūb,* 53; Ibn Abī al-Dunyā, *Al-Riqqah wa al-bukā',* 48; al-Ghazālī, *Iḥyā' 'ulūm al-dīn,* 1:349; Ibn Rajab, *Laṭā'if al-ma'ārif,* 14.
49. Seventy times: al-Bayhaqī, *Shu'ab al-īmān,* 6623. One hundred times: Muslim, 2702 #41.

until his heart no longer enjoins the good and objects to the reprehensible." After [saying] this, the Prophet ﷺ read: "No! Their deeds have cast a veil over their hearts" (Q83:14).[50]

50. With the exception of the part concerning enjoining the good and forbidding evil: Aḥmad bin Ḥanbal, *Al-Musnad,* §7952; Ibn Mājah, 4244; al-Ḥākim, *Al-Mustadrak,* 6; Ibn Abī al-Dunyā, *Al-Tawbah,* 198.

32

GRABBING ATTENTION WHILE NEGLECTING THE SELF

Among the infamies of the soul is its love for talking about people. [This includes] being absorbed in subtleties of knowledge in order to catch the hearts of the gullible, and using one's eloquent speech to turn people towards him [with their attention].

This condition is treated by one acting according to what one preaches, and that one preach to people via his deeds – not his words. It was related that Allah Glorious and Most High revealed to ʿĪsā ibn Maryam (peace be upon him), "When you want to preach to people, [first] preach to yourself. If you respond to your own preaching, then preach to others; and if not, be shy from Me."[51]

---

51. Al-Istānbūlī, *Rūḥ al-bayān,* 4:175, 4:494; al-Aṣbahānī, *Ḥilyat al-awliyā',* 2:382; Ibn Abī al-Dunyā, *Al-Amr bi-l-maʿrūf wa al-nahī ʿan al-munkar,* 97; Shams al-Dīn Muḥammad al-Safīrī, *Al-Majālis al-waʿẓiyyah,* 2:141–42; Aḥmad bin Ḥanbal, *Al-Zuhd,* 300; al-Māwardī, *Adab al-dīn wa al-dunyā,* 33–34; al-Qushayrī, *Al-Risālah al-Qushayriyyah,* 2:369; al-Ghazālī, *Iḥyā' ʿulūm al-dīn,* 1:63, 2:312, 2:330, 4:416; al-Shaʿrānī,

[It is related] that the Prophet ﷺ said, "On my Night Journey I passed people whose lips were being sheared off with shears made of fire. I asked, 'O my brother Jibrīl. Who are they?' He replied, 'Those are the sermonizers from your community [*ummah*] [who] command people and forget themselves even though they read the Book.'"[52]

Al-Ṭabaqāt al-kubrā, 1:98; Ibn Rajab, *Laṭā'if al-ma'ārif,* 18; al-Safārīnī, *Ghidhā' al-albāb*, 1:218.

52. Shams al-Dīn Muḥammad al-Safīrī, *Al-Majalis al-wa'ẓiyyah,* 2:142.

33

JOY, HAPPINESS, AND DEMANDING COMFORT

Among the infamies of the soul is its happiness, joy, and demanding comfort. These are among the results of heedlessness.

This condition is treated by [the soul] waking up to what lies ahead [in the Afterlife]; knowing the individual's shortcomings in what He ordered and his pursuit of what is forbidden. [Its treatment includes] the soul knowing that this abode is his prison, and there is no happiness nor rest in a prison. The Prophet ﷺ said, "This world is the believer's prison and the disbeliever's paradise,"[53] so it is necessary that one's life in this world be the life of the imprisoned, not the life of those seeking comfort. It is related from Dāwūd al-Ṭā'ī that he said, "Brokenheartedness (lit. severing the heart's blood vessels) never ends for those who have knowledge of Allah [*ʿārif*]."

A man asked Bishr al-Ḥāfī, "Why is it that I see you sorrowful?" He replied, "Because things are demanded of me [to perform] and I have no excuse [for neglecting them]."

---

53. Muslim, 2956 #1.

34

FOLLOWING CAPRICE

Among the infamies of the soul is following its caprice, being content with whatever pleases it, and pursuing its desires.

This condition is treated by what Allah Most High ordered in His saying, "and curbed their souls' passions" (Q79:40), and His saying, "The soul does indeed incite to evil" (Q12:53). It was related from Muḍar al-Dārī that he said: "Carving a mountain using your finger tips is easier than going against caprice when it has settled in the soul."

35

INCLINING TOWARDS FELLOWSHIP

Among the infamies of the soul is its inclining towards fellowship with friends and keeping company with brothers.

This condition is treated by the individual knowing that companions depart and that fellowship has separations. It was related from the Prophet ﷺ that Jibrīl (peace be upon him) said to him ﷺ, "Live as you wish, for you are dead. Love whomever you wish, for you will depart him. Do whatever you wish, for you are recompensed for it. Know that a Muslim's nobility is his standing [in prayer] at night, and his strength is being self-sufficient [from other than Allah]."[54]

Abū al-Qāsim al-Ḥakīm said, "All friendship is enmity unless it is sincere. Accumulating wealth is grief, unless it is shared. Company causes confusion unless it treats [an affliction]."

---

54. Ibn Jārūd al-Ṭayālisī, *Musnad Abī Dāwūd al-Ṭayālisī*, 1862; al-Ṭabarānī, *Al-Muʿjam al-awsaṭ*, 4278, 4845; al-Ḥākim, *Al-Mustadrak*, 7921; al-Bayhaqī, *Shuʿab al-īmān*, 10057–58.

36

VIGOR IN OBEYING AND APPROVING OF IT

Among the infamies of the soul is its yearning to be obeyed and regarded as perfect.

This condition is treated by knowing that the soul's deeds – even if sincere – are defective and are not free from defects. The individual should know that he will never make the soul's actions sincere except by ceasing to regard its deeds as perfect.

37

FOLLOWING LUSTS

Among the infamies of the soul is that it reduces the self by following lusts, and if it is allowed to become set in doing this it reduces [acts of] obedience and conforming [to commands].

This condition is treated by denying the soul its desires, inducing it to perform what it dislikes, and contravening it in its demands – since this is what will remove from it its lusts. It was said to Abū Ḥafṣ, "What brings about rectifying the soul?" He said: "Contradicting it, since it is the location of every ruin."[55]

---

55. I have not located a source for this statement.

38

FEELING SECURE FROM SATAN

Among the infamies of the soul is that it feels safe from Satan's plotting, seduction, and whispers.

This condition is treated by rectifying slave-hood according to its conditions, and beseeching Allah to bestow this upon him, since Allah Most High says, "Indeed, you [Satan] have no power over My slaves" (Q15:42).

39

RIGHTEOUSNESS WITHOUT SINCERITY

Among the infamies of the soul is feigning righteousness without demanding sincerity from the heart in the righteousness that it feigns.

This condition is treated by abandoning visible humility except to the degree of inward humiliation in one's heart and conscience, since the Prophet ﷺ said, "Feigning [to have] something you have not been given is like wearing two false garments."[56]

56. Al-Bukhārī, 5219; Muslim, 2129 #126, 2130 #127.

40

BLINDNESS OF ALLAH'S RESPITE

Among the infamies of the soul is a lack of reflection on what the individual sees of Allah granting him respite for his sins.

This condition is treated by [having] perpetual fear. The individual should know that this respite is not from disregard, and that Allah Most High will interrogate him about this and will recompense him for it unless He grants him mercy. Reflection is for those who fear [Allah], because Allah Most High says, "In this there is a lesson for he who fears" (Q79:26).

Someone said:

Her Maker's respite deluded her
    Do not consider her respite as
    [Him] disregarding her!

41

SPREADING INFAMIES OF OTHERS

Among the infamies of the soul is its love to divulge the infamies of one's brothers and companions.

This condition is treated by the individual making himself an exemplar, and loving for people what he loves for himself. [It is] just as it was related from the Prophet ﷺ that he said, "The Muslim is the one who desires for his brother that which he desires for himself," and [it was related] from him ﷺ that he said, "Whoever veils the shame of his Muslim brother, Allah will veil his shame."[57]

57. See #13.

42

LACK OF VIGILANCE

Among the infamies of the soul is neglecting to demand more from one's self concerning one's actions and statements, and being content with what one's soul is doing.

This condition is treated by the individual demanding an increase in [the quality and then the quantity of] his actions and statements, and by following the Forebears.

ʿAlī ibn Abī Ṭālib (Allah be well pleased with him) said, "Whoever is not in excess is deficient."[58]

---

58. I cannot find it attributed to or through ʿAlī (may Allah be pleased with him). But I did find it attributed the Prophet ﷺ: al-Sakhāwī, *Al-Maqāṣid al-ḥasanah,* 1080 – who says the chain is weak; Abū Layth al-Samarqāndī, *Tanbīh al-ghāfilīn,* 592. And I also found it attributed to someone other than the Prophet ﷺ in a dream: Ibn Abī al-Dunyā, *Al-Manāmāt,* 243; Mullā ʿAlī al-Qārī, *Al-Asrār al-marfūʿah,* 328.

43

DENIGRATION AND ARROGANCE

Among the infamies of the soul is denigrating Muslims, deeming itself above them, and being arrogant towards them.

This condition is treated by returning to modesty, and believing in the sanctity of Muslims.[59]

Allah Most High said to His Prophet ﷺ, "So pardon them and ask forgiveness for them and consult with them in the conduct of [communal] affairs" (Q3:159). Know that arrogance is what put Iblīs (accursed is he) in the state wherein he said, "I am better than him. You created me of fire while him you created of clay" (Q38:76).

The Prophet ﷺ looked to the Kaʿba and said, "How great you are, and how great your sanctity! [But] believers have even greater sanctity with Allah than you! Indeed, Allah declared one thing from you sacrosanct, while He declared three things from

59. One should believe that all human beings are owed a certain degree of honor by default. Perhaps the author's qualification is due to it being the most likely case for his audience.

the believers sacrosanct: his blood, his property, and his dignity."[60]

60. Al-Bayhaqī, *Shuʿab al-īmān,* 6280. A slightly shorter version that does not specify there being three things (but still lists them) is in Ibn Mājah, 3932. An even shorter version that mentions only two things being sacrosanct is in al-Tirmidhī, 2032; and Ibn Ḥibbān, 5763.

44

LAZINESS AND DISREGARD FOR THE LAW

Among the infamies of the soul is laziness and abstaining from orders.

This condition is treated by the individual knowing that he is ordered directly by Allah Most High, so the joy of this propels him to have vigor when executing orders. I also heard my grandfather Ismāʿīl ibn Nujayd (may Allah grant him His mercy) say, "Negligence towards orders is from a lack of knowledge of the Commander [*al-Āmir*]."[61]

61. Al-Istānbūlī, *Rūḥ al-bayān,* 10:29; al-Bayhaqī, *Al-Zuhd al-kabīr,* #755; al-Sulamī, *Ṭabaqāt al-ṣūfiyyah,* 341–41.

45

DONNING THE GARB OF THE RIGHTEOUS

Among the infamies of the soul is that it dresses itself in the garb of the righteous while performing the deeds of the immoral.

This condition is treated by abandoning external adornment until one rectifies the interior. [Its treatment includes that] when the individual dons the garb of a people, he strives to conform to their good characteristics and deeds – all or some of them. This is because it is related in the non-prophetic accounts [*khabar*]: "It is sufficient evil for a person that he shows people that he fears Allah while his heart is corrupt."[62]

Abū ʿUthmān said, "External adornment while acting immorally produces persisting [in disobedience]."[63]

62. I have not located a source for this statement.
63. I have not located a source for this statement.

46

SQUANDERING TIME

Among the infamies of the soul is that it squanders its time being occupied with what is not the individual's concern. [This preoccupation] includes the affairs of this world and being engrossed in it with its people.

This condition is treated by the individual knowing that his time is the thing dearest to him. He occupies it with the dearest thing of all: remembrance of Allah, Mighty and Majestic; and constantly obeying Him, and demanding sincerity from his soul. [This is] since it was related from the Prophet ﷺ, "Leave that which causes you doubt for that which does not cause you doubt."[64] The Prophet ﷺ said, "Part of a person perfecting his Islam is leaving that which does not concern him,"[65] and whoever leaves what does not concern him becomes occupied with that which is his concern.

Al-Ḥusayn ibn Manṣūr [al-Ḥallāj] said, "Pay attention to your soul: if you do not occupy it, it will occupy you."[66]

---

64. Al-Tirmidhī, 2518; al-Nasā'ī, 5711.
65. See also #22.
66. Ibn Taymiyyah, *Al-Ḥasanah wa al-sayyi'ah*, 95; Ibn

47

ANGER

Among the infamies of the soul is anger.

This condition is treated by inducing the soul to be content with the decree [of Allah], since anger is a burning ember from Satan. A man came to the Prophet ﷺ and said, "Advise me." He replied ﷺ, "Do not get angry." The man repeated it a second and third time, and he replied ﷺ, "Do not get angry."[67]

Anger takes the servant to the verge of destruction when it is not accompanied by restraint and prohibition from Allah Most High.

Taymiyyah, *Majmūʿ al-fatāwā,* 14:335; al-Ghazālī, *Iḥyāʾ ʿulūm al-dīn,* 4:75; al-Khaṭīb al-Baghdādī, *Tārīkh Baghdād,* 8:710; al-Dhahabī, *Tārīkh al-Islām,* 7:23; al-Dhahabī, *Siyar aʿlām al-nubalāʾ,* 11:213, 11:216, 14:345, 14:350; al-Shaʿrānī, *Al-Ṭabaqāt al-kubrā,* 1:93.

67. Al-Bukhārī, 6116.

48

LYING

Among the infamies of the soul is lying.

This condition is treated by inducing the soul to tell the truth, and abandoning being occupied with people's contentment and hatred. The liar is propelled to lie out of seeking people's acceptance or adorning [oneself] for them in order to gain prestige with them. It was related that the Messenger of Allah ﷺ said, "Truth guides to piety, and piety guides to Paradise; lying guides [to immorality, and immorality guides to] the fire."[68]

68. Al-Bukhārī, 6094; Muslim, 2607 #103, 2607 #105.

49

STINGINESS AND MISERLINESS

Among the infamies of the soul is stinginess and being miserly; both are products of loving this world.

This condition is treated by the individual knowing that this world is paltry and that it will cease to exist. [The individual must know that] its lawful is [a cause for being] accounted for, and its unlawful is [a cause for] torture. It was related from the Prophet ﷺ that he said, "Love of this world is the root of every mistake."[69]

Indeed, Allah Most High informed about this world, [saying:] that it is an illusory delight – so do not be miserly or stingy with it, strive to give freely of it, and do not retain any of it except the amount needed for one's time.

The Prophet ﷺ said, "O Bilāl: Do not fear decrease from He [who is Lord] of the Throne."[70]

---

69. Aḥmad bin Ḥanbal, *Al-Zuhd*, 475; al-Ḥārith al-Muḥasibī, *Adāb al-nufūs*, 136; Ibn Abī al-Dunyā, *Al-Zuhd*, 9, 33, 51, 497; Ibn Abī al-Dunyā, *Dhamm al-dunyā*, 9, 33, 416; al-Daynūrī, *Al-Mujālisah wa jawāhir al-ʿilm*, 985; al-Bayhaqī, *Shuʿab al-īmān*, 9974.
70. Aḥmad bin Ḥanbal, *Al-Zuhd*, 46, 403; al-Ṭabarānī,

50

ITS DISPOSITION FOR FANCIES

Among the infamies of the soul is its disposition for fancies.

This condition is treated by the individual deeming [his] death near, and knowing that one of the Forebears said, "Allah does not want that anyone feels secure from Him in any circumstance, so be wary of Him in all circumstances."

Al-Muʿjam al-awsaṭ, 2572; al-Bayhaqī, *Shuʿab al-īmān,* 1283, 1393, 3067.

51

BEING DELUDED BY FALSE PRAISE

Among the infamies of the soul is being deluded by false praise.

This condition is treated by the individual not being deceived by the words of people – especially given the knowledge one possesses of his [own] soul, and since only he, not them, knows the truth of the matter – when their praise for him disagrees with what Allah Most High knows about him and what he knows about himself. Their praise for him with other than what Allah knows about him and what he himself knows about his soul will not save him from dishonor, so it does not delude him.

52

AVARICE

Among the infamies of the soul is avarice.[71]

This condition is treated by the individual knowing that by his avarice he will not bring about an increase in the sustenance Allah has destined for him. It is just as Ibn Masʿūd related: that the Prophet ﷺ said that Allah Most High says to the angel, "Write his sustenance, his time of death, deeds, and whether damned [in the Fire] or saved [in Paradise]."[72]

Allah Most High says, "My word cannot be changed, nor am I unjust to My servants" (Q50:29).

71. See also #24.
72. Al-Bukhārī, 3208; Muslim, 2643 #1.

53

ENVY

Among the infamies of the soul is envy.

This condition is treated by knowing that the envier is an enemy of the blessing of Allah,[73] and that the Prophet ﷺ said, "Do not envy one another, do not have enmity towards one another; be – O servants of Allah – brothers [to one another]."[74]

Know that envy causes the envier to have little compassion for Muslims.

---

73. cf al-Qushayrī, *Al-Risālat al-Qushayriyya*, 73.
74. Al-Bukhārī, 6064-66, 6076; Muslim, 2559, 2563, 2564.

54

PERSISTING IN A SIN WHILE FANCYING MERCY

Among the infamies of the soul is persisting in committing a sin while fancying forgiveness and expecting mercy.

This condition is treated by one knowing that Allah has made His forgiveness obligatory for those who do not persist in a sin [in the verse] where He says, "and who will not knowingly persist [in misdeeds]" (Q3:135). Abū al-Ḥafṣ said, "Persisting in committing a sin is from being heedless of the power of Allah Most High."

[Its treatment includes] that one knows that Allah Most High has made mercy obligatory for the righteous since He said, "Surely, the mercy of Allah is near to those who act with excellence" (Q7:56). And He made forgiveness obligatory for the repentant when He said, "ask forgiveness of your Lord, then repent to Him" (Q11:52).

55

UNWILLINGLY PERFORMING ACTS OF OBEDIENCE

Among the infamies of the soul is not voluntarily responding to acts of obedience.

This condition is treated by hunger, thirst, traveling, and inducing the soul to do what it dislikes. I heard Manṣūr ibn ʿAbd Allāh say: I heard my paternal uncle from Bisṭām say: I heard my father say:

> A man asked my father Abū Yazīd [al-Bisṭāmī] may Allah sanctify his soul, "What is the most difficult thing you encountered on the path to Allah?" He replied, "It cannot be described!"
>
> Then the man asked, "What is the most insignificant thing you encountered on the path to Allah?" He replied, "It cannot be described."
>
> He then asked, "What is the most difficult thing you encountered from your soul during the path to Allah?" He said, "It cannot be described!"

He asked, "What is the most insignificant thing you encountered from your soul during the path to Allah?" He said, "As for this, yes: I called my soul to one of the various acts of obedience and it did not respond to me voluntarily. And so I forbade it [the self] water for one year."[75]

75. Al-Qushayrī, *Al-Risālah al-Qushayriyyah,* 1:58; Abū Saʿīd al-Khādimī, *Barīqah Muḥammadiyyah,* 2:38–39; Ibn Khalikān, *Wafayāt al-aʿyān,* 2:531; Ibn Mulaqqin, *Ṭabaqāt al-awliyāʾ*, 399.

56

AVARICE AND BEING TIGHTFISTED

Among the infamies of the soul is its avarice through saving and being tightfisted [from others].

This condition is treated by the individual knowing that the soul is not safe from his life ending and that his death is near. Thus, one saves only to the extent he is certain to live and withholds only as long as he will be alive. Saving for someone who cannot secure even a single breath is delusion, and withholding from others in spite of the ensuing consequences is ignorance. This is especially so, considering that it is related from the Prophet ﷺ that he said, "To which of you is the property of your inheritors more beloved to you than your property?" They replied, "There is no one among us except his property is more beloved to him than the property of his inheritors." And he said, "Your property is what precedes you and the property of your inheritors is what remains after you."[76]

76. Al-Bukhārī, 6442.

57

ACCOMPANYING THE REBELLIOUS

Among the infamies of the soul is its accompanying those who diverge from, and rebel against, the truth.

This condition is treated by returning to accompanying those who conform to Allah [*al-Ḥaqq*] and those advancing towards Allah [*al-Ḥaqq*]. The Prophet ﷺ said, "Whoever resembles a people is one of them."[77] And he ﷺ said, "Whoever increases a people's ranks is one of them."[78]

One of the Forebears said, "Accompanying evil people leads to assuming evil in those who are good."[79] [Another] said, "When hearts grow distant from Allah Most High, they detest those who uphold the rights of Allah Most High."[80]

---

77. Abū Dāwūd, 4031.
78. Al-Māwardī, *Adab al-dīn wa al-dunyā,* 149; al-Ghazālī, *Iḥyā' ʿulūm al-dīn*, 2:142.
79. Al-Sulamī, *Al-Waṣiyyah,* 43; al-Māwardī, *Adab al-dīn wa al-dunyā,* 168; al-Qushayrī, *Al-Risālah al-Qushayriyyah,* 2:460; Ibn al-Mufliḥ, *Al-Ādāb al-sharʿiyyah,* 1:49; Abū Saʿīd al-Khādimī, *Barīqah Muḥammadiyyah,* 3:96; 3:130.
80. Attributed to Dhū al-Nūn al-Miṣrī. Ibn ʿAsākir, *Tārīkh*

58

HEEDLESSNESS

Among the infamies of the soul is heedlessness.

This condition is treated by the individual knowing that [Allah] is not heedless of him, since Allah Most High says, "*Your Lord is not unaware of what you do*" (Q11:123). [Its treatment includes] knowing that he is held accountable for notions and aspirations. Whoever realizes this becomes vigilant of his time and attentive to his states; this will remove heedlessness from him.

Dimashq, 45:62; Ibn Mulaqqin, *Ṭabaqāt al-awliyā'*, 226–7.

59

IDLENESS BY FEIGNING RELIANCE ON ALLAH

Among the infamies of the soul is forsaking [or] desisting the pursuit of [one's means of] livelihood, in order to show people that he desisted out of reliance [in Allah], and then expecting sustenance and becoming angry when sustenance does not come to him.

This condition is treated by the individual adhering to pursuing his means of livelihood – because of what was related from the Prophet ﷺ that he said, "The most wholesome thing a man eats is from his [own] work."[81] [And it is treated by] him visibly pursuing a livelihood while inwardly relying upon Allah, this way he appears to pursue a livelihood with people while actually relying upon Allah. This is a level [reserved] for men and the path of the sincere.

81. Ibn Mājah, 2137; Abū Dāwūd, 3528; al-Nasāʾī, 4449, 4451–52.

60

DEPARTING KNOWLEDGE FOR FEIGNED ACHIEVEMENTS

Among the infamies of the soul is fleeing from what manifest knowledge makes obligatory upon him, to claims [of accomplishment] and [inward] states.

This condition is treated by adhering to knowledge, since Allah Most High says, "if you have a dispute concerning any matter, refer it to Allah and the Messenger" (Q4:59), and He said, "O you who believe! Obey Allah and obey the Messenger and those of you who are in authority" (Q4:59). The Prophet ﷺ said, "Seek knowledge, even in China,"[82] and he ﷺ said, "Seeking knowledge is obligatory for every male and female Muslim."[83]

82. Al-Bayhaqī, *Shuʿab al-īmān*, #1543 – all its various transmissions are weak.
83. Al-Suyūṭī, *Al-Durur al-muntathirah*, 283. Without "... and female Muslim": Ibn Mājah, 224.

61

PRIDE IN WHAT IT GIVES

Among the infamies of the soul is that it aggrandizes what it gives and expends, and reproaches its recipient.

This condition is treated by the individual knowing that he [merely] delivers to others their [appointed] sustenance. In reality the sustainer and the giver is Allah, and the individual is a means between slaves and Allah. There is no pride in delivering a right to its rightful owner.

62

SHOWING NEED WHILE HAVING ENOUGH

Among the infamies of the soul is displaying need while having enough.

This condition is treated by the individual feigning sufficiency even though one has [too] little. I heard my grandfather (may Allah grant him His mercy) say, "People used to enter *taṣawwuf* as wealthy people, and become poor while [still] displaying wealth to people. In this time they enter *taṣawwuf* as poor people, become wealthy, and then display poverty to people."

63

DEEMING ITSELF SUPERIOR

Among the infamies of the soul is seeing the individual's superiority over his peers.

This condition is treated by the individual's knowledge of his soul – and no one is more knowledgeable of it than he! – and assuming the best concerning his intimates. [One does this] in order to propel him to denigrating his soul and seeing the superiority of his brothers and intimates. However, it is not sound for the individual to do this until after looking at all people with the eye [that sees] superiority while looking at himself with the eye [that sees] inferiority. I heard my grandfather say: I heard Abū ʿAbd Allāh al-Sijzī say: "You have merit [*faḍl*] as long as you do not see your [own] merit. When you see your [own] merit, you have none."[84]

---

84. Al-Sulamī, *Al-Futuwwah*, 74.

64

TOILING FOR ITS HAPPINESS

Among the infamies of the soul is that the soul endures whatever brings it happiness.[85]

This condition is treated by knowing that Allah hates the exultant [overly joyful]. He Most High says, "Exult not; Allah loves not the exultant" (Q28:76).

Among the characteristics of the Prophet ﷺ is that he was continually somber, constantly pondering. The Prophet ﷺ said, "Indeed Allah loves every somber heart."[86]

Mālik ibn Dīnār said: "Indeed, when the heart is free of somberness it comes to ruin, just as a house comes to ruin when it is uninhabited."[87]

---

85. See also #33.
86. Ibn Abī al-Dunyā, *Al-Hamm wa al-ḥuzn*, 2; al-Kharā'iṭī, *I'tilāl al-qulūb*, 7; al-Ṭabarānī, *Musnad al-shāmiyyīn*, 1480, 2012; Ibn 'Adī al-Jurjānī, *Al-Kāmil fī du'afā' al-rijāl*, 2:210; al-Ḥākim, *Al-Mustadrak*, 7884.
87. Al-Kharā'iṭī, *I'tilāl al-qulūb*, 1:18; *Al-Majālisah wa jawāhir al-'Ilm*, 6:297; al-Aṣbahānī, *Ḥilyat al-awliyā'*, 2:360; al-Bayhaqī, *Shu'ab al-īmān*, 3:295, §1689; Ibn Abī al-Dunyā, *Al-Hamm wa-l-Ḥuzn*, 32, §8; *Al-Zuhd*,

65

IGNORANCE OF ITS CREATOR'S BLESSING

Among the infamies of the soul is that the individual is in a situation befitting gratitude towards Allah, while it assumes the individual is in a station of being patient.

This condition is treated by perceiving the blessings of Allah during all circumstances. I heard Saʿīd ibn ʿAbd Allāh say: "I heard my paternal uncle say: I heard Abū ʿUthmān say: 'People in their entirety are with Allah Most High in the station of gratitude, while they [falsely] assume that they are in the station of patience.'"[88]

259, §1870; *Rawḍat al-ʿUqalāʾ*, 28; al-Qushayrī, *Al-Risālah al-Qushayriyyah*, 1:267; Ibn al-Jawzī, *Ṣifat al-ṣafwah*, 2:167; Abū Saʿīd al-Khādimī, *Barīqah Muḥammadiyyah*, 3:98; Ibn ʿAsākir, *Tārīkh Dimashq*, 56:414–15; al-Dhahabī, *Tārīkh al-Islām*, 3:488; al-Dhahabī, *Siyar aʿlām al-nubalāʾ*, 5:363.

88. Attributed to Abū ʿUthmān al-Maghrebī. Al-Istānbūlī, *Rūḥ al-bayān*, 9:197–98.

66

GRASPING AT DISPENSATIONS

Among the infamies of the soul is reaching for a dispensation using questionable means.

This condition is treated by avoiding obscurities [and knowing] that they lead to doing the unlawful. Do you not see that the Prophet ﷺ said [in] the hadith, "The lawful is clear and the unlawful is clear. Between them lie obscurities; whoever avoids them keeps his religion and reputation safe, and whoever falls into them has fallen into the Fire. It is like the shepherd who [herds] around the sanctuary and being on the verge of trespassing. Indeed, every king has a sanctuary, and the sanctuary of Allah is His prohibitions."[89]

89. Al-Bukhārī, 52, 2051; Muslim, 1599 #107.

67

DISREGARDING LAPSES

Among the infamies of the soul is that it [causes him to] disregard himself when he stumbles, makes a mistake, or the like.

This condition is treated by the individual making amends for the lapse by seeking pardon and quickly repenting so that the soul does not get accustomed to mistakes and the like. I heard ʿAbd Allāh ibn Muḥammad al-Rāzī say: I heard Abū ʿUthmān say, "The tribulation of novices [*murīd*] in general is their disregarding a mistake or offense that happens for them, and forsaking to treat it during its time until the soul becomes accustomed to this and it slips from [the first rank in the path:] the rank of seeking [*irāda*]."[90]

90. Al-Bayhaqī, *Al-Zuhd al-kabīr,* 334.

68

BEING DECEIVED BY MIRACLES

Among the infamies of the soul is being deceived by [evidentiary] miracles.

This condition is treated by the individual knowing that most miracles are deceptions and lures. Allah Most High says, "[And those who deny Our signs] We shall lead them on from whence they know not" (Q7:182).

One of the Forebears said, "Miracles and [divine] assistance are the subtlest things through which the friends of Allah [*awliyā'*] are duped."[91]

---

91. I have not located a source for this statement.

69

SITTING WITH THE RICH

Among the infamies of the soul is its love for sitting with the rich, inclining towards them, running towards them, and honoring them.

This condition is treated by the individual sitting with the poor, knowing that nothing [the rich] possess will reach him except the portion Allah has decreed for him, and so he ceases expecting [something] from them. This causes his love for and inclination towards them to cease. And [its treatment is] that one knows that Allah reproached His Prophet ﷺ about sitting with the poor: "As for him who feels he needs nothing, to him you attend. You are not to blame if he does not purify himself. But as for him who hastens to you, And is in fear [of Allah], You attend not to him" (Q80:5–10). After that the Prophet ﷺ said, "[My] resurrection is [with] your resurrection, and [my] death is [with] your death,"[92] and he said to the poor, "I was ordered to make myself be patient with you."[93]

He ﷺ said, "O Allah! Bring me to life impov-

92. Muslim, 1780 #84, #86; Ibn Ḥibbān, 4760.

93. "...with you": al-Ṭabarānī, *Al-Muʿjam al-ṣaghīr,* 1074. "...with them": Abū Dāwūd, 366; al-Ṭabarānī, *Al-Muʿjam al-awsaṭ,* 8866.

erished, bring me to death impoverished, and resurrect me with the ranks of the poor."[94]

The Prophet ﷺ said to ʿAlī (May Allah ennoble his countenance) and to others (Allah be well pleased with them all), "It is incumbent upon you to love the poor and draw near to them."[95]

94. Al-Tirmidhī, 2352; Ibn Mājah, 4126.
95. Aḥmad bin Ḥanbal, *Al-Musnad*, 21415; Ibn Ḥibbān, 449.

CONCLUSION

In these sections, I have clarified some of the infamies of the soul. From them the rational person can infer what lies behind it, and whomever Allah has granted success and firmness can extricate [themselves] from the soul – in spite of [my] confirmation that it is not possible to completely encompass its infamies. How would that be possible, when the soul is disgraceful in all of its attributes and is not free from a single infamy?! And how is it possible to exhaustively enumerate the infamies of something all of which is an infamy. Indeed, Allah Most High has described the soul in that it is the one inclined towards evil![96] This aside, perhaps the slave can rectify some of the soul's infamies through these treatments, and thereby free himself from some of its infamies.

May Allah Most High grant us success in following the right way, and remove from us notions of heedlessness and lust. May He put us under His flank, custody, protection, and attention. Indeed, He is the one capable of this, the one who grants it, and who gives freely of His mercy and His grace. May the prayers of Allah be upon Muḥammad, the Prophet, and upon his pure folk.

96. Quran, 12:53.

REFERENCES

ʿAbd al-Karīm bin Hawāzin bin ʿAbd al-Malik al-Qushayrī (465 AH). *Al-Risālat al-Qushayriyyah*. Edited by ʿAbd al-Ḥalīm Maḥmūd and Maḥmūd bin al-Sharīf. Cairo: Dār al-Maʿārif.

ʿAbd al-Raḥmān bin Abī Bakr Jalāl al-Dīn al-Suyūtī (911 AH). *Al-Durr al-manthūr fī al-tafsīr bi-l-maʾthūr*. Beirut: Dār al-Fikr, n.d.

ʿAbd al-Wahhāb bin Aḥmad bin ʿAlī al-Shaʿrānī (973 AH). *Al-Ṭabaqāt al-kubrā* (*Lawāqiḥ al-anwār fī ṭabaqāt al-akhyār*). Cairo: Maktabat Muḥammad al-Mulayjī al-Kutubī wa Akhīhi, 1315.

Abū Aḥmad bin ʿAdī al-Jurjānī (365AH). *Al-Kāmil fī ḍuʿafāʾ al-rijāl*. Edited by ʿĀdil Aḥmad ʿAbd al-Mawjūd, ʿAlī Muḥammad Muʿawwaḍ, and ʿAbd al-Fattāḥ Abū Sunnah. Beirut: Al-Kutub al-ʿIlmiyyah, 1997/1418.

Abū al-Fadāʾ Ismāʿīl bin ʿUmar bin Kathīr (774 AH). *Al-Bidāyah wa al-nihāyah*. Beirut: Dār al-Fikr, 1986/1407.

Abū al-Faḍl Zayn al-Dīn ʿAbd al-Raḥīm al-ʿIrāqī (806 AH). *Al-Mughnī ʿan ḥaml al-asfār fī al-asfār fī takhrīj mā fī Al-Iḥyāʾ min al-akhbār.* Beirut: Dār Ibn Ḥazm, 2005/1426.

Abū al-Ḥasan Nūr al-Dīn ʿAlī bin Abī Bakr bin Sulayman al-Haythamī (807 AH). *Ghāyat al-maqṣad fī zawāʾid al-Musnad.* Edited by Khalāf Maḥmūd ʿAbd al-Samīʿ. Beirut: Dār al-Kutub al-ʿIlmiyyah, 2001/1421.

Abū al-Ḥasan Nūr al-Dīn ʿAlī bin Abī Bakr bin Sulayman al-Haythamī (807 AH). *Majmaʿ al-zawāʾid wa manbaʿ al-fawāʿid. Edited by Haṣām al-Dīn al-Qudsī.* Cairo: Maktabat al-Qudsī, 1994/1414.

Abū al-Ḥasan ʿAlī bin ʿUmar al-Dāraquṭnī (385 AH). *Al-ʿIlal al-wāridah fī aḥādīth al-nabawiyyah.* Edited by Maḥfūẓ al-Raḥmān Zayn Allah al-Salafī. Volumes 1–11: Riyadh: Dār Ṭayyibah, 1985/1405. Volumes 12–15: Dammam: Dār Ibn al-Jawzī, 1427.

Abū al-Layth Naṣr bin Muḥammad bin Aḥmad al-Samarqandī (373 AH). *Tanbīh al-ghāfilīn ba-aḥādīth Sayyid al-anbīyāʾ wa al-mursalīn.* Edited by Yūsuf ʿAlī Badawī. Beirut: Dār Ibn Kathīr, 2000/1421.

Abū al-Qāsim Ḥamzah bin Yūfuf bin Ibrāhīm al-Jurjānī (427 AH). Edited by Muḥammad ʿAbd al-Muʿīn Khān, et al. Beirut: ʿĀlim al-Kutub, 1987/1407.

Abū al-Qāsim ʿAlī bin al-Ḥasan bin Hibbat Allāh ("Ibn ʿAsākir"). *Tārīkh Dimashq*. Edited by ʿAmr bin Ghurāmah. Beirut: Dār al-Fikar, 1995/1415.

Abū al-ʿAbbās Aḥmad bin Muḥammd bin Mahdī bin ʿAjībah (1224 AH). *Al-Baḥr al-madīd fī tafsīr al-Qurʾān al-majīd*. Edited by Aḥmad ʿAbd Allah al-Qurashī Ruslān. Cairo: distributed by Doctor Ḥasan ʿAbbās Zakī, 1419.

Abū Al-ʿAbbās Shams al-Dīn Aḥmad bin Muḥammad, Ibn Khalikān (681 AH). *Wafāyāt al-aʿyān*. Edited by Iḥsān ʿAbbās. Beirut: Dār Ṣādir, n.d.

Abū Bakr Aḥmad bin Marwān al-Daynūrī al-Mālikī (333 AH). *Al-Mujālisah wa jawāhir al-ʿilm*. Edited by Abū ʿUbaydah Mashhūr bin Ḥasan Āl Salmān. Beirut: Dār Ibn Ḥazm, 1419.

Abū Bakr Aḥmad bin ʿAlī bin Thābit bin Aḥmad bin Mahdī al-Khaṭīb al-Baghdādī (463 AH). *Al-Muntakhab min kitāb al-Zuhd wa al-raqāʾiq*. Edited by ʿĀmir Ḥasan Ṣabrī. Beurit: Dār al-Bashāʾir al-Islāmiyyah, 2000/1420.

———. *Tārīkh Baghdād*. Edited by Bashshār ʿAwwād Maʿrūf. Beirut: Dār al-Gharb al-Islāmī, 2002/1422.

Abū Bakr bin Abī Shaybah (235 AH). *Al-Kitāb al-Muṣannaf fī al-aḥādīth wa al-āthār.* Edited by Kamāl Yūsuf al-Ḥūt. Riyadh: Maktabat al-Rushd, 1409.

Abū Bakr Muḥammad bin Abī Isḥāq bin Ibrāhīm bin Yaʿqūb al-Kalābādhī (380 AH). *Baḥr al-fawāʾid (maʿānī al-akhbār)*. Edited by Muḥammad Ḥasan Muḥammad Ḥasan Ismāʿīl, Aḥmad Farīd al-Mazīdī. Beirut: Dār al-Kutub al-ʿIlmiyyah, 1999/1420.

Abū Bakr Muḥammad bin Hārūn al-Rūyānī (307 AH). *Musnad al-Rūyānī.* Edited by Ayman ʿAlī Abū Yamānī. Cairo: Muʾassisah Qurṭubah, 1416.

Abū Bakr Muḥammad bin Jaʿfar al-Kharāʾiṭī (327 AH). *Iʿtilāl al-qulūb.* Edited by Ḥamdī al-Damardāsh. Riyadh: Maktabah al-Mukarammah, 2000/1421.

Abū Bakr ʿAbd Allāh bin Muḥammad bin ʿUbayd bin Sufyān ("Ibn Abī al-Dunyā") (281 AH). *Al-Amr bi-l-maʿrūf wa al-nahī ʿan al-munkar.* Edited by Ṣalāḥ bin ʿIyāḍ al-Shalāḥī. n.a.: Maktabat al-Ghurabāʾ al-Athariyyah, 1997/1418.

———. *Al-Ikhlāṣ wa al-niyyah*. Edited by Iyād Khālid al-Ṭabbāʿ. Damascus: Dār al-Bashāʾir, 1413.

———. *Al-Manāmāt*. Edited by ʿAbd al-Qādir Aḥmad ʿAṭāʾ. Beirut: Muʾassisah al-Kutub al-Thaqāfiyyah, 1993/1413.

———. *Al-Mutamannīn*. Edited by Muḥammad Khayr Ramaḍān Yūsuf. Beirut: Dār Ibn Ḥazm, 1997/1418.

———. *Al-Qināʿah wa al-taʿafuf*. Edited by Muṣṭafā ʿAbd al-Qādir ʿAṭāʾ. Beirut: Muʾassisah al-Kutub al-Thaqāfiyyah, 1993/1413.

———. *Al-Riqqah wa al-bvukāʾ*. Edited by Muḥammad Khayr Ramaḍān Yūsuf. Beirut: Dār Ibn Ḥazm, 1998/1419.

———. *Al-Ṣamt wa adab al-lisān*. Edited by Abū Isḥāq al-Ḥuwaynī. Beirut: Dār al-Kutub al-ʿIlmiyyah, 1410.

———. *Dhamm al-ghībah wa al-namīmah*. Edited by Bashīr Muḥammad ʿUyūn. Damascus: Dār al-Bayān, 1992/1413.

Abū Dāwūd Sulaymān bin Dāwūd bin al-Jārūd al-Ṭayālisī (204 AH). *Musnad Abī Dāwūd al-Ṭayālisī*. Edited by Muḥammad bin ʿAbd al-Muḥsin al-Turkī. Egypt: Dār Hijr, 1999/1419.

Abū Ḥāmid Muḥammad bin Muḥammad al-Ghazālī (505 AH). *Iḥyāʾ ʿulūm al-dīn*. Beirut: Dār al-Maʿrifah, n.d.

Abū Muḥammad ʿAbd al-Ḥumayd bin Ḥamīd (249 AH). *Al-Muntakhab min Musnad ʿAbd bin Ḥumayd*. Edited by Muṣṭafā al-ʿAdawī. Dār Balansiyyah li-l-Nashr wa-l-Tawzīʿ, 2002/1423.

Abū Muḥammad ʿAbd Allāh bin Muḥammad bin Jaʿfar bin Ḥayān al-Anṣārī ("Abū al-Shaykh al-Aṣbahānī") (369 AH). *Kitāb al-amthāl fī ḥadīth al-nabawī*. Edited by ʿAbd al-ʿAlī ʿAbd al-Ḥamīd Ḥāmid. Bombay: al-Dār al-Salafiyyah, 1987/1408.

Abū Naʿīm Aḥmad bin ʿAbd Allāh bin Aḥmad al-Aṣbahānī (430AH). *Ḥilyat al-awliyā' wa Ṭabaqāt al-Aṣfiyā'*. Al-Saʿādah, 1974/1394.

Abū Shujʿah al-Daylamī al-Hamadhānī (509 AH). *Al-Firdaus bi-maʿthūr al-khiṭāb*. Edited by al-Saʿīd bin Basyūnī Zaghlūl. Beirut: Dār al-Kutub al-ʿIlmiyyah, 1986/1406.

Abū Zakhariyā Yaḥyā bin Maʿīn bin ʿAwn bin Ziyād bin Busṭām bin ʿAbd al-Raḥmān (233 AH). *Tārīkh Ibn Maʿīn (Riwāyat al-Dūrī)*. Edited by Aḥmad Muḥammad Nūr Sayf. Mecca: Markaz al-Baḥth al-ʿIlmī wa Iḥyā' al-Turāth al-Islāmī, 1979/1399.

Abū ʿAbd al-Ḥākim Muḥammad bin ʿAbd Allāh (405 AH). *Al-Mustadrak ʿalā al-Ṣaḥīḥayn.* Edited by Muṣṭafā ʿAbd al-Qādir ʿAṭāʾ. Beirut: Dār al-Kutub al-ʿIlmiyyah, 1990/1411.

Abū ʿAbd Allāh Aḥmad bin Muḥammad bin Ḥanbal (241 AH). *Musnad al-Imām Aḥmad bin Ḥanbal.* Edited by Shuʿayb al-Arnāʾūṭ, et al. Beirut: Muʾassisat al-Risālah, 2001/1421.

Abū ʿAbd Allāh Muḥammad bin Abī Naṣr Futūḥ bin ʿAbd Allāh al-Ḥamīdī (488 AH). *Akhbār wa ashʿār li-Abī ʿAbd Allāh al-Ḥamīdī ʿan Shuyūkhihi.* Edited by Khalāf Maḥmūd ʿAbd al-Samīʿ. Beirut: Dār al-Kutub al-ʿIlmiyyah, 2002/1423.

———. *Al-Tadhkirah li-l-Ḥamīdī.* Edited by Khalāf Maḥmūd ʿAbd al-Samīʿ. Beirut: Dār al-Kutub al-ʿIlmiyyah, 2002/1423.

Abū ʿAbd Allāh Muḥammad bin Khalaf bin Ḥafṣ al-ʿAttār al-Dūrī (331 AH). *Mā rawāhu al-akābir ʿan Mālik bin Anas.* Edited by ʿAwwād al-Khalafj. Beirut: Muʾassisah al-Rayān, 1416.

Abū ʿAbd Allāh Muḥammad bin Salāmah bin Jaʿfar bin ʿAlī al-Qaḍāʿī (454 AH). *Musnad al-Shihāb.* Edited by Ḥamdi bin ʿAbd al-Majīd al-Salafī. Beirut: Muʾassisah al-Risālah, 1986/1407.

Abū ʿAmr Yūsuf bin ʿAbd Allāh bin Muḥammad bin ʿAbd al-Barr (463 AH). *Jāmiʿ bayān al-ʿilm wa faḍlihi*. Edited by Abū al-Ashbāl al-Zuhayrī. Saudi Arabia: Dār Ibn al-Jawzī, 1994/1414.

Aḥmad bin al-Ḥussein bin ʿAlī bin Mūsā al-Bayhaqī (458 AH). *Al-Asmāʾ wa al-ṣifāt*. Edited by ʿAbd Allāh bin Muḥammad al-Ḥāshidī. Jeddah: Maktabat al-Sawādī, 1993/1413.

———. *Kitāb al-zuhd al-kabīr*. Edited by ʿĀmir Aḥmad Ḥaydar. Beirut: Muʾassisah al-Kutub al-Thaqāfiyyah, 1996.

———. *Shuʿab al-īmān*. Edited by ʿAdb al-ʿAlī ʿAbd al-Ḥamīd Ḥāmid. n.a: Maktabat al-Rushd, 2003/1423.

ʿAlī bin Muḥammad al-Mullā al-Qārī (1014 AH). *Al-Asrār al-marfūʿah fī al-akhbār al-mauʿḍūah*. Edited by Muḥammad al-Ṣabbāgh. Beirut: Muʾassisah al-Risālah, n.d.

Al-Ḥārith bin Asad al-Muḥāsibī (243 AH). Ādāb al-Nufūs. Edited by ʿAbd al-Qādir Aḥmad ʿAṭāʾ, Beirut: Dār al-Jayl, n.d.

Ḥussein bin Muḥammad bin al-Ḥasan al-Diyār Bakrī (966 AH). *Tārīkh al-khamīs fī aḥwāl anfus al-nafīs*. Beirut: Dār Ṣādir, n.d.

Al-ʿIrāqi (806 AH), Ibn al-Subkī (771 AH), al-Zabīdī (1205 AH). *Takhrīj aḥādīth Iḥyā ʿulūm al-dīn*. Riyādh: Dār al-ʿĀṣimah li-l-Nashr, 1987/1408.

Ibn Mulaqqin Sirāj al-Dīn Abū Ḥafṣ ʿUmar bin ʿAlī bin Aḥmad al-Shāfiʿī (804 AH). *Ṭabaqāt al-awliyāʾ*. Edited by Nūr al-Dīn Shuraybah. Cairo: Maktabat al-Khānjī, 1994/1415.

Ismāʿīl bin Muḥammad bin ʿAbd al-Hādī al-Jarrāḥī al-ʿAjlūnī (1162 AH). *Kashf al-khafāʾ wa muzīl al-ilbās*. Edited by ʿAbd al-Ḥamīd bin Aḥmad bin Yūsuf bin Hindāwī. Maktabat al-ʿAṣriyyah, 2000/1420.

Ismāʿīl Ḥaqqī bin Muṣṭafā al-Istānbūlī (1127 AH). *Rūḥ al-bayān*. Beirut: Dar al-Fikr, n.d.

Jamāl al-Dīn Abū al-Faraj ʿAbd al-Raḥmān bin ʿAlī bin Muḥammad al-Jawzī (597 AH). *Al-ʿIlal al-mutanāhiyyah fī aḥadīth al-wāhiyyah*. Edited by Irshād al-Ḥaqq al-Atharī. Faysalabad: Idārat al-ʿUlūm al-Athariyyah, 1981/1401.

———. *Al-Tabṣirah*. Beirut: Dār al-Kutub al-ʿImiyyah, 1986/1406.

———. *Ṣifat al-ṣafwah*. Edited by Aḥmad bin ʿAlī. Cairo: Dār al-Ḥadīth, 2000/1421.

Muḥammad Amīn bin Faḍl Allāh bin Muḥibb al-Dīn bin Muḥammad (1111 AH). *Khulāṣat al-athar fī aʿyān al-qarn al-ḥādī ʿashr*. Beirut: Dār al-Ṣādir, n.d.

Muḥammad bin Abī Bakr bin Ayūb bin Saʿd Shams al-Dīn Ibn Qayyim al-Jawziyyah (751 AH). *Shifāʾ al-ghalīl fī masāʾil al-qaḍāʾ wa al-qadar wa al-ḥikmah wa al-taʿlīl.* Beirut: Dār al-Maʿrifah, 1978/1398.

———. *Ṭarīq al-hijratayn wa bāb al-saʿādatayn.* Cairo: Dār al-Salafiyyah, 1394.

Muḥammad bin al-Ḥussein bin Muḥammad bin Mūsā bin Khālid bin Sālim al-Naysabūri, Abū ʿAbd al-Raḥmān al-Sulamī (412 AH). *Al-Futuwwah.* Edited by Iḥsān Dhanūn al-Thāmirī and Muḥammad ʿAbd Allāh al-Qadḥāt. Amman: Dār al-Rāzī, 2002/1422.

———. *Ṭabaqāt al-ṣūfiyyah.* Edited by Muṣṭafā ʿAbd al-Qādir ʿAṭā. Beirut: Dār al-Kutub al-ʿIlmiyyah, 1998/1419.

———. *Waṣiyyat al-Sheikh al-Sulamī.* Edited by Majdī Fatḥī al-Sayyid. Tanta: Maktabah al-Ṣaḥābah, n.d.

Muḥammad bin Ḥibbān bin Aḥmad bin Ḥibbān, Abū Ḥātim al-Dārimī al-Bustī (354 AH). *Rawḍat al-ʿuqalāʾ wa nuzhat al-fuḍalāʾ.* Edited by Muḥammad Muḥyi al-Dīn ʿAbd al-Ḥamīd. Beirut: Dār al-Kutub ʿIlmiyyah, n.d.

Muḥammad bin Ismāʿīl bin Ibrāhīm al-Bukhārī (256 AH). *Al-Adab al-mufrad.* Edited by Muḥammad Fuʾād ʿAbd al-Bāqī. Beirut: Dār al-Bashāʾir al-Islāmiyyah, 1989/1409.

Muḥammad bin Mufliḥ bin Muḥammad bin Faraj (763 AH). *Al-Ādāb al-sharʿiyyah wa al-manaḥ al-marʿiyyah*. n.a.: ʿĀlim al-Kutub, n.d.

Muḥammad bin Muḥammad bin Muṣṭafā bin ʿUthmān (1156 AH). *Burīqah Muḥammadiyyah fī sharḥ ṭarīqat Muḥammadiyyah wa sharīʿah nabawiyyah fī asīrah Aḥmadiyyah*. n.a.: Maṭbah al-Ḥalabī, 1348.

Nūr al-Dīn ʿAlī bin Muḥammad bin ʿAlī bin ʿAbd al-Raḥmān Ibn ʿIrāq al-Kanānī (963 AH). *Tanzīh al-sharīʿah al-marfūʿah ʿan akhbār al-shanīʿah al-mawḍūʿah*. Edited by ʿAbd al-Wahhāb ʿAbd al-Laṭīf, ʿAbd Allāh Muḥammad Ṣiddīq al-Ghamārī. Beirut: Dār al-Kutub al-ʿIlmiyyah, 1399.

Shams al-Dīn Abū al-Khayr Muḥammad bin ʿAbd al-Raḥmān bin Muḥammad bin Abī Bakr al-Sakhāwī (902 AH). *Al-Ḍawʾ al-lāmiʿ li-ahl al-qarn al-tāsiʿ*. Beirut: Dār Maktabah al-Ḥayāh, n.d.

———. *Al-Maqāṣid al-ḥasanah fī bayān kathīr min aḥādīth al-mushtaharah ʿalā al-alsinah*. Edited by Muḥammad ʿUthmān al-Khasht. Beirut: Dār al-Kitāb al-ʿArabī, 1985/1405.

Shams al-Dīn Abū al-ʿAwn Muḥammad bin Aḥmad bin Sālim al-Safārīnī (1188 AH). *Ghidhāʾ al-albāb*. Egypt: Muʾassissah Qurṭubah, 1993/1414.

Shams al-Dīn Abū ʿAbd Allāh Muḥammad bin Aḥmad bin ʿUthmān al-Dhahabī (748 AH). *Mīzān al-iʿtidāl fī naqd al-rijāl*. Edited by ʿAlī bin Muḥammad al-Bujāwī. Beirut: Dār al-Maʿrifah, 1963/1382.

———. *Siyar aʿlām al-nubalāʾ*. Edited by Shuʿayb al-Arnāʾūṭ, et al. Amman: Muʾassisah al-Risālah, 1985/1405.

———. *Tarīkh al-islām*. Edited by Bashshār ʿAwwād Maʿrūf. Beirut: Dār al-Gharb al-Islāmī, 2003.

Shams al-Dīn Muḥammad bin ʿAmd al-Safīrī (956 AH). *Al-Majālis al-waʿẓiyyah fī sharḥ Khayr al-Bariyyah ﷺ min Ṣaḥīḥ al-Imām al-Bukhārī*. Edited by Aḥmad Fatḥī ʿAbd al-Raḥmān. Beirut: Dār al-Kutub al-ʿIlmiyyah (2004/1425).

Sulaymān al-Ṭabarānī (360 AH). *Al-Muʿjam al-awsaṭ*. Edited by Ṭāriq bin ʿIwaḍ Allāh bin Muḥammad and ʿAbd al-Muḥsin bin Ibrāhīm al-Ḥusayni. Cairo: Dār al-Ḥaraman, n.d.

———. *Al-Muʿjam al-ṣaghīr*. Edited by Muḥammad Skakūr Maḥmūd al-Ḥājj Amrīr. Beirut: al-Maktab al-Islāmī, 1985/1405.

Sulaymān bin Aḥmad bin Ayūb bin Muṭīr al-Lakhmī, Abū Qāsim al-Ṭabarānī (360 AH). *Al-Duʿāʾ*. Edited by Muṣṭafā ʿAbd al-Qādir ʿAṭāʾ. Beirut: Dār al-Kutub al-ʿIlmiyyah, 1413.

———. *Musnad al-shāmiyyīn*. Edited by Ḥamdī bin ʿAbd al-Majīd al-Salafī. Beurit: Mu'ssisah al-Risālah, 1984/1405.

Taqi al-Dīn Abū al-ʿAbbās Aḥmad bin ʿAbd al-Ḥalīm bin Taymiyyah (728 AH). *Al-Ḥasanah wa al-sayʾiyah*. Beirut: Dār al-Kutub al-Ilmiyyah, n.d.

———. *Al-ʿUbūdiyyah*. Edited by Muḥammad Zuhayr Shāwīsh. Beirut: al-Maktab al-Islāmī, 2005/1426.

———. *Jāmiʿ masāʾil li-Ibn Taymiyyah*. Edited by Muḥammad ʿAzīz Shams. Dār al-ʿĀlim al-Fūʾād li-l-Nashr wa-l-Tawzīʿ, 1422.

———. *Majmūʿ al-fatāwā*. Edited by ʿAbd al-Raḥmān bin Muḥammad bin Qāsim. Medina: Majmaʿ al-Malak Fahd li-l-Ṭibāʿah al-Maṣḥaf al-Sharīf, 1995/1416.

Yaḥyā bin al-Ḥussayn bin Ismāʿīl bin Zayd al-Ḥasanī al-Shajarī (499 AH). *Tartīb al-Amālī al-khumaysiyyah li-l-Shajarī*. Edited by Muḥammad Ḥasan Muḥammad Ḥasan Ismaāʿīl. Beirut: Dār al-Kutub al-ʿIlmiyyah, 2001/1422.

Zayn al-Dīn Muḥammad ("ʿAbd al-Raʿūf") bin Tāj al-ʿĀrifīn al-Manāwī (1041 AH). Egypt.: al-Maktabah al-Tijāriyyah al-Kubrā, 1356.

Zayn al-Dīn ʿAbd al-Raḥmān bin Aḥmad bin Rajab (795 AH). *Faḍl ʿIlm al-salaf ʿalā al-khalaf*.

———. *Laṭāʾif al-maʿārif*. Beirut: Dār Ibn Ḥazm, 2004/1424.

Also from Islamosaic

Connecting with the Quran

Etiquette with the Quran

Hadith Nomenclature Primers

Hanbali Acts of Worship

Ibn Juzay's Sufic Exegesis

Sharḥ Al-Waraqāt

Supplement for the Seeker of Certitude The Accessible Conspectus

The Encompassing Epistle

The Evident Memorandum

The Refutation of Those Who Do Not Follow the Four Schools

The Ultimate Conspectus

ISLAMOSAIC

WWW.ISLAMOSAIC.COM

Printed in Great Britain
by Amazon

37062003R00073